I0134576

Seven Principles of Wellness:

Healing Your Mind, Body and Spirit Through Ayurveda

Also by Omileye Achikeobi-Lewis, M.Ed

My first two books in life were written under my middle name Ezolaagbo

A Journey Through Breath
I Pray for Healing
Seven Principles of Wellness
In the Spirit of Wellness
Dreamtime Awakening
Ploop: An Abundant Pregnancy Journey
Rainbow Goddess
Beautiful Waters

see also:
Omileye's work at yeyeosun.com

A Naked Truth Book
UK, United States

A Naked Truth Book
P. O. Box 461
South Carolina, SC 29720
www.aharalife.com

Copyright © 2009, 2016, Omileye Achikeobi-Lewis
Design by: Adaugo Joseph & L. Derrick Lewis
Editor: L. Derrick Lewis
Assistant Editor: Remah Joseph

All rights reserved. This book or parts thereof, may
Not be reproduced in any form without permission

This book is printed in the United States of America
August 2009, reprinted December 2017

Library of Congress Control Number: 2009908399

Thanks to the:

Creator
Ancestors
Great Mother
Mother Nature
Family members: Remah Joseph (mum), Derrick Lewis (husband),
-Jeffrey Joseph (brother), and Kem Ra Joseph-Achikeobi-Jess (son), Omololu
Achikeobi-Lewis

A special thanks to my husband for his tireless help with the editing.

Table of Contents

Introduction
The Awakening

*"When my daughter was seven years old, says artist
Howard Ikemoto, "she asked me one
day what I did at work. I told her
I worked at the college that my
job was to help people how to draw. She
stared back at me, incredulous, and said, "you mean they
forget"*

The Transformation Journey Awakens

It is my sincere belief that everyone can live a balanced and harmonious life. It is also my sincere belief that life puts many challenges in our way to bring out our greatness. I also have a further belief that we live in a time when it is important to understand, what those many generations before us understood, there are age old principles which can help us obtain the balance of Mind, Body, and Soul that we desire and absolutely deserve.

These beliefs have driven the fabric of my life. They are the beliefs of seeing a humanity which is joyous, creative, optimistic, well, and in harmony with every aspect of life. Secretly I really want to transform the whole world to authentic balanced living. Call this a high ambition, but what is living without it and let's face it our Personal Legend comes with us when we are born. Our job is to actualize it.

I have been living from the foundation of my Personal Legend for over fifteen years now. One day I remember waking up and just knew I wanted to help women and individuals live their more joyous life. I had spent years transforming my life and now wanted to pass on some of the lessons. I began with the successful *Journey Through Breath* Workshops, wrote a well received book by the same title (writing it was made a little easier by my professional journalistic experience), won a few awards, wrote another book called *I Pray For Healing*, paused a little and got distracted on many occasions, worked in wellness with my mother, gained a second degree in Complimentary Health Sciences (Ayurvedic Medicine – Eastern Medicine). This journey took fifteen years. It was filled with bumps, challenges, doubts, hopes and fear. Yet, all along my Personal legend did not stop pulling me forward by the power of its magnetic force forward.

There were many life changing experiences that have shaped who I am, and how I work with others today. First let's talk about my very first meditation experience. I remember sitting in my meditation class with the soft music of water and drums playing in the background; the even softer voice of our instructor guided us through the rhythmic breathing exercises; and the sudden insperience I had when my breath connected me to my magical center. No words can really describe when what it is like to touch your inner loving core. Maybe, one. One I have learnt in my new home of America – "awesome".

That experience was over twenty years ago in the middle of a cold London winter. It was one of those moments that no one has been able to take away from me. It made me realize I am more than I can see, feel and touch. I am love, perfect balance, wisdom and harmony. I am part of an infinite whole. I realized that being in alignment with our inner loving core is one of the major keys to true happiness. It was an experience I wanted to share with others.

Then there was Sherene Lee. A dynamic sister who walked into my second four week *A Journey Through Breath* workshop. She was hard to miss in her elegant red summer dress that floated in the wind, close cropped hair and Elfin like beauty. As with every participant I wondered what had drawn Sherene to this transformation experience. We were all soon to find out that Sherene was a high powered media person who had breast cancer. One week before coming to the workshop Sherene had discovered a lump in her breast, went to the doctor, discovered it was malignant and the size of a small gulf ball. She was devastated. Her world suddenly felt as though the bottom had fallen out of it. I taught the class the science of calm breathing, letting go of old emotions and then we added visualization work on top of it all. I told Sherene she should lovingly visualize her lump shrinking to the size of a pea. She did. Three weeks after doing this exercise everyday at home Sherene went for her second medical checkup. She was informed by her surprised doctor that her malignant lump had shrunken to the size of a pea. He informed her he had never seen such a thing in the whole of his medical career. He asked her what she had been doing. She answered him honestly, "breathing calmly and visualizing".

Sherene shared her results with the workshop. We were elated. That was when I knew beyond a doubt that the power within us really has the ability to transform our lives for the positive. If only more of us knew how to tap into it. I felt re-confirmed in my desire to help individuals to understand the power of transformation and the principles that bring them about. As my Journey Through Breath workshops continued my work became more in demand. I remember being asked to be a key note speaker at the UK's Royal Festival Hall for the yearly International *Woman's Day event In Celebration of Our Sisters*. I shook like crazy as I spoke to over 3000 women about transformation.

Yet, another huge leap in my transformation work happened when I began my second degree in Ayurvedic Medicine & Complimentary Healthy Sciences at the University of Middlesex (UK). The course was created in partnership with the college of Ayurveda (UK). It was intense, fascinating and taught me that the body is made up of energy, and true balance is keeping this energy in harmony through our diet, lifestyle, and emotions. It was through this course that I discovered the fundamental universal principles of obtaining and keeping perfect harmony and health. It was through my life experiences, and work that I further discovered that following ones personal legend is a fundamental universal principle of good health.

The kindness of my professor Dr. Athique founder of the College of Ayurveda (UK), has touched every aspect of my life, which I pay forward in everything I do. His kindness allowed me to finish my Ayurvedic degree, even though I was financially struggling to pay for the course. He taught me that we do not have to be mean in a mean world.

It was his kindness I carried in my heart as I entered another powerful stage of my transformational work – working with young vulnerable adults from a community that was struggling financially. In Lancaster South Carolina, there was not much to do. Many of the young people of color and others were leaving school without appropriate qualifications to help them gain meaningful employment. My husband Derrick and I began to work with this community, as a result of Dr. Stella Williams and her husband Reverend George Williams founders of the United Heritage Total Family Outreach Coalition (UHTFOC). This dynamic duo were former teachers and well-loved in the community. They had decided to remedy the severe literacy issue in Lancaster by starting UHTFOC. Doing so was a struggle, but they were courageous and willing to go the full mile.

One day Dr. Stella Williams and her husband informed me and Derrick that they would like us to start a wellness program for a group of about 20 young single moms and some young males. At first I was nervous because I knew that these young people would not have been exposed to Ayurveda, wellness, or even meditation. I had no idea how I would teach them these concepts in a way that was meaningful for their lives. After much encouragement from Derrick I eventually designed a 12 week program called *In the Spirit of Wellness based* on *Seven Principles of Wellness*.

It was during the journey of In the Spirit of Wellness with the young adults from UHTFOC, that I had discovered that the deep healing power of Ayurveda can touch anyone's life. When it does it stays with you forever. I was so touched when many of the young adults began to share with Derrick and I that they had been using the techniques with their families. I was even more impressed when one of the students gave news reporter Greg Summers, Feature Editor for the Lancaster News an amazing Ayurvedic Head Massage. At the end of *A Spirit of Wellness* program, I gathered all our experiences up and into a book by the same title. The hope was and still is, that it would help other young people begin their journey to holistic wellness.

My transformation work and journey continue to take me to miraculous and deeper places within myself. In the summer of 2016, I had the greatest fortune to have a private audience with His Holiness the Dalai Lama and his personal Oracle Kuten La, who is also the Tibetan State Oracle. Life and visions of unusually large natural catastrophes led Kuten La to extend a personal invitation for me to see him in Dharamsala, India. It was an arduous hero's journey, which I made with Derrick and my little daughter Omololu. It was one that led to me to discover Kuten La had received the same visions two days before I arrived in Dharamsala. It also led Kuten La to give me a very powerful initiation, and task me with the job of encouraging people to establish a relationship with the Four Elemental Mothers again through actions and ceremonies. Later on he encouraged and gave me his blessings to teach the universal Four Elemental Mother Ceremony and practice, which had flowed through me from the Mother Elements themselves.

Since my journey and meeting with His Holiness the Dalai Lama and Kuten La - the Tibetan State Oracle, my experience with Mother Nature, her internal and external flow have deepened. I am wrapped in her magic almost everyday now. It is this magic I wish to wrap you in – the magic of coming home to yourself and the Mother Elements which sustain the matrix of all of life.

It is my sincere desire that you heal your wounds and come into contact with yourself as a hero, who has made and continues to make difficult and wondrous journeys. I want to cheer you on, as you discover how to live in balance with life and her sacred flow. I want to be there when you smile and discover the powerful luminous light that you are and become engulfed by its infinite wisdom. I want to be there to help you to traverse through the difficulties as you discover the things that block you within. I want to be that good friend who helps you know – you can do this, it's your time.

The Journey Never Ends

I remember once reading somewhere - times are not normal. So forget about being normal, embrace being wild. May *Seven Principles of Wellness* take you on a journey to meet your wild self, the one that has been forgotten along on the way. Just a little peep into your journey chapters:

Principle 1: Awaken Your Journey

In Awaken Your Journey you discover that everything that has happened to your life has been a process of awakening, a trumpet call from your spirit that there are things it needs to get on with, ways it wants to live, unfold, love, cry and be happy. You are encouraged to not just ignore the call to live an authentic life but to embrace it.

Principle 2: Awaken Emotional Bliss

Discover how and why things just seem to keep on happening over and over again in your life like a stuck record; how the things you have not faced up to take on a life of their own and keep on attracting more of the same energy; how to rid yourself of the emotions that keep you from your joy and your authentic self; how to increase the emotions that make you an antennae of abundance; how to use breath, energy balancing, positive affirmations, release, chakra and crystal work to keep the powerful flow from your authentic self going.

Principle 3: Awaken the Inner Eye

In Awaken the Inner Eye you will discover how the universe supports and guides your journey through dreams, synchronicity, and messages. You will also learn how to use the techniques to awaken and deepen your inner intuition and guidance of your authentic self.

Principle 4: Awaken Body Bliss

In Awaken Body Bliss you will discover how to keep your mind, body and soul on track with purpose. You will discover what the messages of your body mean and discover all the ancient principles and routines for mind-body and soul care.

Principle 5: Awaken Body Nourishment

So now you have discovered how to release your emotions, awaken your inner intuition, get your body and mind in top peak conditions – it is time to discover the full low down on the various stages of illness, and how to keep your body totally balanced through creating "good food essence".

Principle 6: Awaken the Mind-Body Type

Your soul journey is enhanced when you discover that each individual has a Mind-Body type which has its own emotional, food, lifestyle and personality type, illness and optimum health. You will discover what your unique Mind-Body type. You will also grasp principles on how to manage, and balance your illness and other imbalances.

Principle 7: Awaken Sacred Balance

Discover more about the sacred elements and how being in touch with nature and Mother Earth can awaken balance, personal power, creativity, and an abundance of love, compassion and gratitude. You will also discover why walking gently on the earth is a must and why a spiritual journey must include an increasing sense of ethics, the four pillars of life, the Five Afflictions.

Be love and be peace,

Yeye Omileye Achikeobi-Lewis, M.Ed
September 2017

Principle 1: Awaken Your Journey

*Nothing has a stronger influence
Psychologically, on their environment
and especially on their children
than the unlived life of the
parent.*

C.G JUNG

The Hero's Journey

Inhale and listen to these words carefully. Embrace them into every fiber of your being. Keep them deep in the chambers of your heart. Nurture them lovingly. Let them empower you and propel you positively forward.

You are more than what you see. You are more than what you feel. Life may have knocked you around a little (okay a lot) but God is not against you. God is for you. Your soul is not against you; it is for you. Life is not your enemy; it is your friend.

Everything that has happened in your life has been for a reason. It has brought you to this place and so far in order for you to know your true power. It has, like a concerned mother, gently and sometimes harshly guided you so that you can be the best of who you came to be. Before you came into this existence you wrote a contract, literally. God and those guides who were to help you through your journey on earth carefully examined it. They ensured that there was nothing in that contract that you could not handle. Nothing in that contract that would take you completly apart. You also had your own exit plan in that contract, the time when you would depart.

Applaud yourself for your decision to come to earth showed courage on your part. As you can see earth is not the easiest learning ground. You are on what the great mythologist Joseph Campbell called, "the hero's journey". The journey where you go out into the world to fetch something that you really need. On the way you meet all sorts of monsters, fairies, and wisdom. You feel somewhat scared, motivated, diffident, exhilarated, and often times out of your league. But you always come back from the journey empowered.

The fact that you are reading the pages of this book means that you are ready to fully embrace the "hero's journey" and awaken to the words of Marianne Williamson,

"Our deepest fear is not that we are inadequate. Our deepest fear is that we are powerful beyond measure. It is our light, not our darkness that most frightens us. We ask ourselves, "Who am I to be brilliant, gorgeous, talented, and fabulous?" Actually, "Who are you *not* to be? You are a child of God. Your playing small does not serve the world. There is nothing enlightened about shrinking so that other people won't feel insecure around you. We are all meant to shine, as children do. We were born to make manifest the glory of God that is within us. It's not just in some of us; it's in everyone. And as we let our own light shine, we unconsciously give other people permission to do the same. As we are liberated from our own fear, our presence automatically liberates others."

Now is a time to be willing to forgive yourself and – like the shepherd boy in the Paulo Coelho's *The Alchemist* keep the oil on the spoon while you look at the pleasures of the world.

The Messenges

Take a deep breath in, hold, and exhale slowly. Now focus your mind on this.

Your inner loving core is always talking to you and guiding you through various messengers of life. It will talk to you through the densest part of spirit, the body. It will also talk to you through your emotions. It will talk to you through a cup, a poster board, and practically anything it can get its hands on you. The inner loving core, ultimately known as the Soul, helps you to tap into the endless stream of and power of universal consciousness in your life.

What are the messages that your inner loving core is sending to you? Be still, because deep down the answer to all your life questions do lie within. Are there things you are not doing? People who need to go? People who need to stay? Boundaries that need to be set? Love that needs to be embraced? Adventures that need to be had? Truths that need to be spoken?

Know that even if you try to deny the truth that lies within there it is a losing battle. Your inner loving core along with universal consciousness will always find a way for you to shine. For everything has a purpose and the purpose of life is to keep on manifesting the full creative beauty and love of the universe. Just look at a flower. It is programmed to bloom and give joy to the world. A plant is programmed to grow and give abundance. A honey bee was created to help give nourishment. You have a purpose, uniqueness and beauty too. Trying to deny this truth or dumb it down with bad food, bad relationships, overworking, playing small in the world will just not work. For you are destined for greatness.

Those aches, pains, arthritis, MS, Sinus problems, skin issues, memory loss, tumors, confusion, weight issues, money problems, anxiety, bad relationships, depression, anger are all somehow connected to realities that need to be embraced and things that just need to go. Acquiring wealth is all well and good but it cannot replace the fact that your inner loving core will always strive for true peace, love, abundance, harmony and fulfillment of creative purpose. You are destined for greatness but not with a large bag bumping over your shoulders; and definitely not while caught up in another's dreams, drama and purpose.

There is an ancient Yoruba story that tells us when the world is falling apart. The divine spirits who were sent to inhabit the world originally were having a good time. They forgot all about the laws of God. They also forgot to respect the female Goddess that came with them. But during their good times they had plundered the earth. Disease, famine, sickness and chaos became the order of the day. The men began to panic. They went to every divinity they could think of to get the answers to saving the world. No one could help them. They did not think about going to the Goddess for any answers. They had no respect for her. They thought "what does she know". They went back to heaven for the solution. God told the panicked divinities, "I have given all the wisdom of the world to the woman. It is from her you have to get the answers".

They went back to the female Goddess and indeed through her the day was saved. This story sounds very much like the world we live in today. The Goddess represents the sacred energy of water, the inner sacred, love, beauty, wisdom, self nurturing, living higher. She symbolizes the only way to save our inner and outer worlds and to restore their beauty is to go back to love and the inner most sacred. Despite the fact, the men had treated her so bad the Goddess was not angry with them. She forgives them for their ignorance. So she also represents the fact that we too must learn to forgive others and ourselves in order to heal.

Many people who read this ancient story often do not see the lessons that it holds for global healing. Our global crisis is ultimately a statement on the state of our inner humanity. It is a statement on how far we have traveled away from our inner most sacred. So what is the answer? I believe the answer lies in going back to the qualities that the Goddess in the story represents: wisdom, balance, compassion, love, divine creative purpose, grace, reverence and inner sacredness.

I think situations such as global warming are telling us "cut it whichever way you want - you have to heal your inner humanity, get your soul back on track, and ultimately return back to our inner most sacred. There is no other way." I once remember a well known South Carolina Naturalist, Rudy Mancke telling an audience that I was part of, "if people would just realize there is a world outside of themselves, which needs them, they would not be so depressed and self centered. They would realize they are part of something so much bigger than just their own bodies. When they do their lives would feel so much more joyful." I am inclined to agree with him.

Water Crystals

Dr. Masaru Emoto, author of several books including The True Power of Water" was awarded the Humanity4Water award from the Humanity4Water project founded by my husband and myself.

We gave him this award because we were truly impressed by his contribution in the area of water and the healing of humanity. Dr. Emoto is an internationally renowned Japanese researcher and forward thinker who showed how love, gratitude, forgiveness and positive intentions truly do heal all ails. He has spent years of his life devoted to the study of water. He found a way with the help of scientist Ishibashi to photograph water crystals. He took samples of water from all over the world and discovered that water from different countries and areas within those countries formed different crystals. The purer the water the more beautiful the crystals formed.

Mr. Emoto's discoveries led him to believe that water receives and takes in information. So he began to take samples of water and label them with different messages. He found that the samples labeled "love and gratitude" formed beautiful bold crystals like "flowers in full bloom". While samples labeled "anger" and other negative words formed ugly shapes instead of impressive crystals. His work led him to draw one of the conclusions that since human beings are 70% water then we must definitely be affected by the messages we take in through thoughts, words and deeds.

He further realized that water was affected by the subtle energy known as Hado (universal consciousness). Through a Hado machine, a radionic machine, which measured vibrations at a cellular level he conducted a Hado examination on over 100 people. In this examination he measured the Hado of each individual regarding the most commonly shared emotions (thirty-eight traits including stress, worry, pressure, irritability, perplexity and excess fear) and then he checked which part of their body resonated the most with each emotion. He discovered that those who feel stress tend to have problems with their intestines. Worries are often expressed as problems in the cervical nerves, feelings of irritability in the parasympathetic division of the autonomic nerve system, excess fear in the kidneys and anxiety in the stomach.

By using the Hado machine Emoto discovered that a negative emotion could be over ridden by a positive emotion thus aiding in the healing of the physical illness associated with the negative emotion. Read the chart on the following page to discover which emotion is affecting your body according to the Mr. Emoto's Hado experiment.

My son conducted the same experiment for his Science Project at A.R Rucker School in South Carolina. He was trying to prove the hypothesis that "Water is Alive", after being told that water was not by his science teacher. My husband and I joined him in the experiment. It was conducted over a period of three weeks. We each portioned of rice cooked in the same pot into two separate bottles of the same size. One was sent love and the other hate. Within a few days the "hate rice" was filled with black fungi and began to smell badly. But the "Love rice" stayed white. By the end of the three weeks the "hate rice" was completely black and the "love rice" was still white with only a little bit of green fungi and no smell of rotting.

In fact, something strange happened to the "love rice". It began to emit a sweet smell. The teachers were fascinated by the results. Something even stranger happened.

Months later both the "hate rice" and "love rice" which are still on his display board have retained their forms. At the end of the experiment my son said, "mummy, you know what's funny? The hate rice looks like how I feel inside when people say cruel things to me."

What is the point of sharing all of this – I think to show that: we are affected by the amount of positive and negative feelings we have in our lives and direct at others; we can create a more abundant reality; our bodies always reflect the state of our internal experiences and emotions.

Feet on Earth and Head in Sky

I remember once reading Yoga Master B.K.S Iyengar's take on the reality of being human. In his book *Light on Life* he stated "we human beings live between the two realities of earth and sky. The earth stands for all that is practical, material, tangible, and incarnate. It is the knowable world, objectively knowable through voyages of discovery and observation." While the sky symbolizes all that is perfect, Omniscient (all knowing), Omnipresent (all wise), and Omnipotent (all powerful). He advised that the way to live your best life is to harmonize these two worlds.

His beliefs are shared by many leading thinkers. In the 1950's Dr Maslow lead the way in Humanistic Psychologists. He believed that every person has a strong desire to realize his or her full potential, to reach a level of Self-actualization. To prove that humans are not simply blindly reacting to situations, but trying to accomplish something greater, Maslow studied mentally healthy individuals instead of people with serious psychological issues. This enabled him to discover that people experience "peak experiences", high points in life when the individual is in harmony with himself and his surroundings. Self-actualized people can have many peak experiences throughout a day while others have those experiences less frequently.

Maslow created a visual aid that explained his theory. He called it the *Hierarchy of Needs*. It is a pyramid depicting the levels of human needs, psychological and physical. Maslow discovered that when a human being ascends the steps of the pyramid he reaches self actualization. At the bottom of the pyramid are the "Basic needs or Physiological needs" of a human being, food and water and sex. The next level is "Safety Needs: Security, Order, and Stability." These two steps are important to the physical survival of the person. Once individuals have basic nutrition, shelter and safety, they attempt to accomplish more. The third level of need is "Love and Belonging," which are psychological needs; when individuals have taken care of themselves physically, they are ready to share themselves with others. The fourth level is achieved when individuals feel comfortable with what they have accomplished. This is the "Esteem" level, the level of success and status (from self and others). The top of the pyramid, "Need for Self-actualization," occurs when individuals reach a state of harmony, peace, understanding.

Together we will journey and you will discover all the elements to living more holistically and in harmony with your true sense of self.

Maslow's Table of *Hierarchy of Needs.*

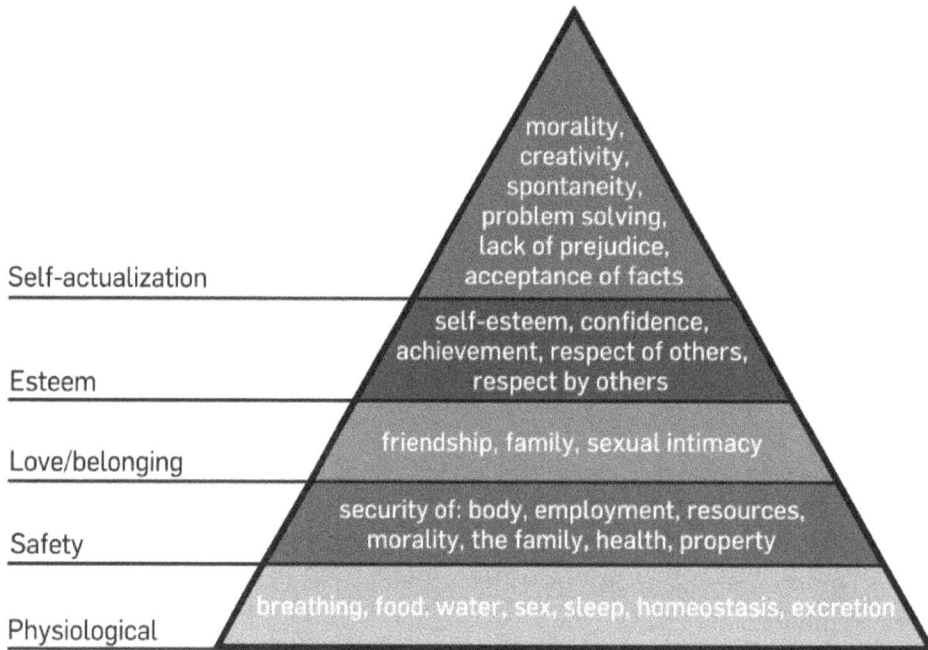

Self-actualization — morality, creativity, spontaneity, problem solving, lack of prejudice, acceptance of facts

Esteem — self-esteem, confidence, achievement, respect of others, respect by others

Love/belonging — friendship, family, sexual intimacy

Safety — security of: body, employment, resources, morality, the family, health, property

Physiological — breathing, food, water, sex, sleep, homeostasis, excretion

Dr. Emoto's Chart of Emotions

Which emotions are giving you what messages? *(With a few of my own findings added indicated with an *.)*

Emotion	Main organs that resonate with emotions of disease	Hado of disease	Canceling emotion (can be done by saying the word)
Stress	Intestines	Indigestion	Relaxation
Worry	Cervical nerves	Stiff shoulders	Easy going
Perplexity	Autonomic nerves	Low-back pain	Good grace
Excess fear	Kidneys	Renal disease	Peace of mind
Anxiety	Stomach	Dyspepsia	Relief
Anger	Liver	Hepatitis	Compassion
Apathy	Spine	Weekend vitality	Passion
Impatience	Pancreas	Diabetes	Tolerance
Loneliness	Brains hippo campus	Senile dementia	Pleasure
Sadness	Blood	Leukemia	Joy
Grudge	Skin	Skin ulceration	Gratitude
Parental Anger *	Womb	Fibroids or ovary issues	Forgiveness
Feeling unloved or unworthy*	Fat	Weight	Love
Vulnerable*	Skin	Skin rashes and ailments	Supported
Fear of moving forward*	Knees, legs	Painful joints, injuries	Life flows easily
Overwhelmed by life burdens*	Shoulders, back	Pains	Supported and love

Exercise

Claiming Your Life

1. Are you ready to take ownership of your life and make a transformation?
2. Create an affirmation that gives you courage to move forward. Remember to keep affirmation in the present. "I am open to love" etc
3. Do some research. Find a story where someone has changed their life around. Know that you can do it to.

Journal Pages

Go confidently in the direction of your dreams! Live the life you've imagined. As you simplify your life, the law of the universe will be simpler.

HENRY DAVID THOREAU

_____

_____

_____

_____

_____

_____

_____

_____

_____

_____

_____

_____

_____

_____

_____

_____

_____

_____

Principle 2: Awaken Emotional Bliss

Your task is not to seek for love, but merely to seek and find all the barriers within yourself that you have built against it.

Rumi

The map of perfect balance

I think I am a little qualified to talk about emotions and how they can inhibit our greatness or release us into it. For much of my life I have lived in a tumultuous emotional world. My journey, like most, has been spent just trying to figure myself and my life purpose out. I have had to constantly battle through the emotions of fear, discontentment and plain frustration at not knowing how this game of life is really suppose to work. Especially, the one on my own tennis court. So many times I felt like the loser in most of my games including my warm up matches!

So what are these emotions of frustration all about? Simply put, it's all about not feeling connected to our inner loving core. I have seen friends have break-downs because they are not feeling connected to their souls. I have seen these same friends, family members and strangers end up doing the wrong things, having the wrong relationships because they are not connected to the feeling of wholeness that lay deep within.

Being disconnected from the depth of your wholeness is the worst feeling ever. It is a great recipe for listlessness and frustration. It can feel like wading in a dark pool that is meant to be clear and light. I think you know what I mean.   So how do we really get into clear water and safely onto dry land? First it helps to understand the world of the Little I.

The Little I

The Little I tries to pretend it's us, our true selves, but it really isn't. It can never stand in for the omniscient, omnipotent, omnipresent soul we have. The Little I promises us great things: wealth, happiness, love, status, great careers but it makes us look for those things in all the wrong place. Then when we are miserable the Little I makes us feel that we are the ones to blame. The Little I is greedy too. It can never be satisfied. It just keeps on wanting more and more. It is also filled with things that you really can do without: jealously, anger, hate, greed and obsessive love. It fills us up with its cocktail of toxicity and tells us "that's just life". By the way the Little I is called ego. It keeps us limited in tiny boxes and away from the circle of greatness.

I remember once reading an article about a very rich man who seemed to live in a very little way. His name was Jean Paul Getty. I found an article on him dated July 1974 on www.people.com. The heading read "World's richest man: At 81, Jean Paul Getty, Who Assembled One of the Oil World's Great Empires, Lives in Elegant Isolation". It was a riveting article. It was clear that Mr. Getty was a dab hand at collecting wealth but not true happiness. Many parts of the article stood out, but this one I would like to quote. It was a comment on how Mr. Getty lived in the last days of his life, in fact in all of his rich life.

"The setting, of course, is what one notices first. Not merely the withered face and the shrunken body too small for his clothes, but his mansion's mausoleum-like ambiance. Seeing the old man in his castle, sealed behind electric gates, ringed by double fences topped with barbed wire and surrounded by bodyguards, 25 prowling attack dogs and a motley, silent retinue of servants, it is hard to remember that Getty is not really a prisoner. Isolated from his family—his oldest son, George, died last year in Los Angeles, and he rarely sees his three other sons—he seems starkly and strangely alone. The 450-year-old mansion itself is drafty, coldly formal and uninviting. Getty's friends try to avoid staying overnight. One unwary visitor who rose during the night to go to a bathroom down the hall was nearly set upon by the guard dogs roaming the corridors."

What Mr. Getty did not know is that the Little I offers things that glitter but they are far from permanent. They are empty fake trinkets filled with promises that echo down lonely hall ways. It is a true pusher of all that will disappoint you in the long run. Believe me when I say, the Little I will fight you when you all the way when you try to get rid of it

The Big I

The Big I is none other than our inner loving core. It is the source of our true identity and the consciousness that guides us with wisdom and love towards purpose. Like a tap when it is turned on it sustains and nourishes every part of our being. It is that voice of reason, joy, abundance, and the source of everlasting happiness. Our inner loving core is the vessel of universal consciousness within each and every one of us. When we live under its loving wings there is no one who can make us feel small again. Even if we feel small for a moment it reminds us with its gentle voice – we are big, bodacious, and beautiful/handsome. All the ancient texts of the world are based on helping us ascend and re-connect to the song of our soul and universe. While the Little I makes you believe wisdom is something outside of yourself; the Big I reminds us that the universe is the abundant store of all knowing. There are many masters out there who can guide us, but even the Buddha had to eventually find enlightenment under a tree and from within his own inner loving core which we ultimately call the soul.

The Path Full of Stones

So if we really are all these great things what happened and what happens? Why do we feel confused, lonely or just lost half the times? The answer lies in the impact life and people have had on us. I know someone who is very smart, very talented, and very funny and only if you knew him you would realize he is also very unsure of himself. He had all the things to make him successful in life but one thing was missing – self love. He came from a large family of women who made the men feel worthless. He also had an extremely manipulative mother who made him feel bad about what his father did to her, and ultimately what "men" did to her. His father had left her with several children while he played around the world. It was sorrowful to see this talented individual believe that he was no good because the women in his life had taught him that men were no good.

I knew another person. A beautiful, very talented, very charming woman who actually ran a successful business, but she did not think she was any of the above things mentioned. Why? Throughout her school years she had been told how stupid she was at math. She grew up in the islands where math is highly valued and creativity is not. So being not so hot at math equated to being plain stupid. We know that is not true, but she was made to believe that.

I also knew a little boy who was incredibly smart but extremely shy because during his school years he had a slight learning difficulty that had not been identified and dealt with properly. This made him feel not as smart or as incredible as the other children. This feeling would have stayed with him for life and he would have grown into one of the many unsure adults we witness in life today if he had not been rescued early.

The list can go on forever. I have dealt with hundreds of clients and even myself. The truth is don't matter how accomplished we seem in the "Little I" things, we are often leaps behind knowing and having a relationship with our inner Self because someone, somewhere made us feel unloved, not smart, not talented, not good enough, not worthy. Those feelings just stayed buried within the memory of our cells, and became part of the fabric of our mind, bodies and actions. I wish it was a little bit more complicated than that but it really isn't. Every painful memory you have had is stored in the hypothalamus. A part of the brain which is in charge with coming up with a solution on how to stop you from getting hurt from similar situations in the future. Unfortunately, there are many situations that can seem like the old thus causing you to constantly repeat behavior that has helped you to avoid the pain you wish to avoid. Therefore it is important on your path to healing that you begin the path to releasing the old habits that keep you stuck in the past. The good news is delivered by Dr. Pascale Michelon who states, "the brain has the amazing ability to The brain has the amazing ability to reorganize itself by forming new connections between brain cells (neurons)." That ability is known as Brain Plasticity.

The Aura of Life

As we said previously – every thought, emotion, and thing in life is made up of energy. Einstein confirmed this when he delivered the formula E=MC2 to the world. One that confirmed from energy comes matter and matter goes back to energy. Einstein's revelation began to move the Western world away from a concept that had predominated since the Age of Enlightenment – reality could be measured in a purely mechanical way. So if once it was believed that we were no more than material atoms and nothing went beyond its physical form. It was now understood that the atom itself was not a solid entity but made up of swirls of energy in motion which became known as atomic clouds. Each atom with its energy state gives of a frequency which has its own colour band.

You know we talk about "I don't like that person's vibe, but I like that person's vibe". Well, we are merely picking up the energy frequency of the person's emotions, thoughts, feelings and experiences. The sum total of the individual's energy frequency surrounds their body as an electro magnetic field. Science confirms everything in life has one. Have you ever seen a picture of the earth's electromagnetic field. It is truly beautiful. It looks like a huge watery tadpole. Some people can see other people's auras. Two people once told me on two separate occasions that I had a blue aura. I was fascinated by this revelation. Proof of the energy field that exist around us was provided by a scientist called Dr. Walter J.Kilner who developed the Kilner screen through which he could see auras.

In 1939 Professor Seymon Kirlian visited a hospital in Russia where he witnessed something interesting. He observed that when glass electrodes were placed close to a patient's skin there was a tiny flash of light. Kirlian was fascinated. He began to do experiments on his own hand. He placed it between two metal plates and took a photograph of what happened when he switched on an electrical current. He managed to do something interesting – capture the outline of his hand surrounded by a corona light. He realized he had photographed his own aura. He went on to develop Kirlian photography which captures the electromagnetic field surrounding a person.

As we saw earlier the sum total of all our experiences, emotions and feelings are stored deep within our memories and cells. Which in turn are held within our auric electromagnetic field. So if you are looking for love, but deep down you believe love hurts you will attract a hurtful and abusive person in your life. You will notice that this pattern keeps on repeating itself over and over again. I remember I once had a client called Joan. Joan could not seem to find the right partner. She was tall, beautiful and quite a catch. But there was no love in her life. However, she had life experiences that taught her that she was not worthy. Every time, she attracted a partner into her life he seemed to be abusive. She was puzzled. She came to me looking for a solution to what seemed like a lifelong problem.

I explained to Joan that she was wearing "I am not worthy" message in her auric field.

Through Holistic Counseling and Bio Energy Release & Balancing techniques I helped her to release her painful past. Six weeks latter she found the loving man whom she is now going to marry. Therefore, we can see the importance of clearing those negative experiences from the cache of our beings.

Past Life Experiences and Pain

Not only the immediate past, but the past from way back when can affect our current lives. I These are known as past life experiences. They account for the talents, lessons, some of the people and even some of the illness we often suffer in this lifetime. I became interested in past life experiences when my brother Tony died. The morning after his death, feeling distressed, I went jogging. It was five in the morning and quite dark. However, this did not deter me. I did a few laps around our local Common which was just a five minute walk from our family house. As I neared my final round, small shimmers of light began to break onto the common. I looked over to admire the natural morning beauty of the vast expanse of grass touched by the shards of light. That's when I saw the unexpected - my brother walking towards me. He was wearing the same clothes he had worn the day he had passed. I rubbed my eyes. But my brother kept on walking towards me. He was the only person walking across the Common. I was entranced. How could this be? I thought. He kept on walking towards me and then suddenly he disappeared into the daybreak. It was this incident that made me curious about the issue of what happens to the soul after death. However, it is a curiosity I did not pursue until a second incident happened – the recent passing away of my brother in-law.

My husband was away in the hospital with his mother, father and siblings. I was left in the house of my in-laws alone with my son. While they were away all the phones went down. That had never happened before. With the lines down I had no other way of knowing what was happening at the hospital. Anxious and restless I tried to go to sleep. Eventually as sleep began to set in a rather large body as real as daylight filled the bed. It lay peacefully next to me. I decided not to panic. The body lying next to me was that of my brother in law. He lay there for about fifteen minutes and then I saw his body disappear into tiny dots.

Soon after wards, the phone lines came back on. It was my husband. Before he could say anything I said, "I know, he was lying right next to me. " Apparently, he had passed away a few moments after I saw him fade away. I did not know my brother in law well and in fact I had only met him once. But he was a very loving and compassionate person. He genuinely touched my heart from the moment I encountered him. I knew he wanted my husband to know he was okay, as they were very close.

Books have always played an interesting part in my life. The right ones always seem to come at the right moments. It was a few months after my brother in laws death that I encountered a book called *Saved by the Light by Paul Brinkley. I took the book home* and I read the book in one night. It had me excited. After that I read numerous other books that detailed past life experiences.

My research confirmed that much of our pain is caused by the current past in our present lives (which I knew), or by the past life. The case examples cited by many of the authors were fascinating and you could see how the individuals past life was definitely affecting their present life. It was also interesting that after a past life regression many of the individuals felt almost an immediate relief from life symptoms that had been plaguing them. The traditional notion of Karma is indeed connected to the fact that what we did in our past lives creates our present lives. Our present lives become our past lives which eventually affects the life after it. So the idea is to do lots of good actions, learn your journey lessons well so that you can have a great present life and eventually have no need to incarnate again.

I have done past life regressions on various members of my family, including myself and I have been amazed at how accurate they have been. My thirteen year old son is completely obsessed with Japan. He had a past life experience in Japan which was highly accurate. It was also information that he would not have been able to put together for himself. His experience was highly intricate and it took me a little bit of research to put it all together but it definitely explained his connection with Eastern cultures. I have always suffered from a week back. In one past life experience I was dragged on my back by a jeering crowd in India for harming an abusive husband. I myself have always had a strong connection to Indian spirituality which was also explained in that past life when I saw myself being taught by an Indian sage.

Healing the Wounds

I suppose by now it is clear – healing the wounds of the past is important to experiencing happiness. But, let's be brutally honest about the healing experience. It can feel like a slog. But, oh how great are the rewards. The most important thing on your journey is to be gentle with yourself. Treat yourself like a baby that needs lots of encouragement and gentle guidance to feel welcomed into this world. Know that you are on journey not to become something but to be who you always have been. Nothing is more beautiful than that.

Life Purpose

Painful life experiences are one thing, but the pain of not knowing our life purpose is often a cause of much angst and depression for many. This fact is reflected in Abraham Maslow's pyramid of self actualization created more than 50 years ago. Through much research Dr. Maslow discovered that those who feel purposeful were living at the highest level and qualities that humanity has to offer.

So following your bliss is an absolute must to experiencing happiness in your life. The more you heal is the more you will come into contact with that blissful feeling. But where do you and how do you find purpose? Your purpose is often staring you right in the face. It is hidden in those things you love to do and wrapped up in your life experiences. Quite often in life I have pondered the question "am I on purpose?" Sometimes, I have flights of fantasy about studying for law because I really love law. But, over and over my life keeps on pulling back into the field of human potential, life and earth wellness. Helping people to heal through writing is also an intricate part of my purpose. Recently I embraced this fully. One day I prayed to God to really reveal my purpose. The months that followed saw me writing two books, helping my son to write his, bumping someone who had been incarcerated who happened to want me to read his manuscript, sudden frequent visits to the library and my husband commenting on how much our bedroom was beginning to look like the library. If I did not get the message about my relationship to books then God was surely shouting "do you get it now?"

Don't let fear hold you back from your life purpose. Just remember what Marion Williamson said in her wonderfully uplifting book, *A Course In Miracles*. "Our deepest fear is not that we are inadequate. Our deepest fear is that we are powerful beyond measure".

How do you even know when you are out of purpose? I suppose the answer is "when you just don't feel right with yourself." Emotions are a good barometer to where you are at with self and life in general. I remember once reading the *Artist's Way* by Julia Cameroon. I was interested in her take on the emotion of jealousy. "My jealousy roars in the head, tightens the chest, massages my stomach lining with a cold fist as it searches out the best grip. I have long regarded jealousy as my greatest weakness. Only recently have I seen it for the tough-love friend that it is." She continues to say, "Jealousy is a map. Each of our jealousy maps differs." Jealousies, frustration, disappointment, feeling that someone is better than you, anger at an individual are often road maps to things that are missing from our own life.

Life Stories

So let's get to the crux of the matter. How do we change? Is it even possible to change? The answer is a resounding yes. The mind and body is very self correcting and works hard to help you live out your full glory. To create change it is important to be able to pinpoint the story. When I was a journalist the key to a great story was to find the "angle" of the story. From that everything else flowed. This is the same with our lives. We must find the angle from which everything in our lives is hinging and flowing from. When working with clients much of the deep healing begins right there. Finding the story is a very crucial stage to healing.

As Carl Jung stated, the personal history is "the patient's secret, the rock against which he is shattered. If I know his secret story, I have a key to the treatment."
As a journalist I have always been very good at finding the story. At first I thought it was because I was a good correspondent. Then that ability followed me into my healing work and the rest of my life. That is when I realized it was a gift. I think it is one I inherited from my grandmother and the lineage of women before her.

Everything to do with how your life is today has a story behind it. Be it a small one, medium one or plain gigantic one – it's still a story that has got you to where you are today. I have often found that the answer behind the pain is more times than not a small one. One client's father favored her sister over her. The result – her whole life became filled with the purpose of finding love. Another client had a very bright but angry six year old son. We discovered she had rejected him, without knowing it, from birth. This realization coupled with her son's healing sessions allowed him to heal from his pain.

A strange thing begins to happen as you uncover the story behind your pain things begin to make sense. You begin to see yourself as though for the first time. Your life purpose opens up. It's an amazing phenomenon to behold. I have no true words or explanation for it except to say it appears that the story behind the pain is like dust on a window pane. Imagine the window pane is your soul. As soon as you dust it off you see the glory of the light. A shining soul will always radiate purpose. The client who stopped making her life purpose "looking for love" had been working as a Bank Manager at the time. When she realized the story behind her pain she came into an unexpected discovery – she loved love and wanted to help others find it. The beauty with life – no lesson is wasted. Her love lessons were now going to serve her true soul's purpose to be a relationship counselor. Now I want you to hold on tightly to this point – everything you have been through has been a mere training ground for unfolding your soul purpose. It may be your mission to be a great healer, so you experience a lot of hurt in life to know how to heal it. You may have a calling to be a lawyer so you experience or see injustice that infuriates your spirit. Or you may be called to be a wonderful mother so you suffer at the hands of a mother who is cruel and unfair. She makes you know this is not how you want to be. Everything we experience is like a training ground.

Getting To The Story

So how do you get to the story behind your pain and the story to whom you are suppose to be in life? There are a series of questions that you can ask yourself and this will be covered in the exercise section. But know that most of the self research you will do will be along the lines of uncovering the key incidents that have happened in your life such as the relationship you had with your mother and father, friends etc; how you felt and reacted when these incidents happened. Our life purpose is often staring us right in the faces. It is wrapped up in all the things we love to do. It is also wrapped up in the underlying purpose behind those things. So if you like to cook, make boxes, write poems, write books, create body care products, and heal, what on earth is your life purpose? Just to let you into a little secret. Those are all the things I love to do in life. Underlying all those things is my desire to see people happy.

The Seven Chakras and Emotional Freedom

Once you have unwrapped your life story and the story behind your pain. What do you do then? Well, you begin to release the things you don't need and enhance the things you do. How do you do that? As a healer the most effective way I have found to do this is to understand and tune into the energy system. Remember we mentioned everything is made up of energy, including us. Well, that energy is organized in the Mind-Body system and stored in the major energy centers known as the Chakras.

There are seven major chakras and twenty three minor chakras. Working with the seven major chakras is a major key to quick transformation, emotional freedom and life balance. Each major chakra is intricately connected to the endocrine system which controls key mind/body functions and balance within the body. Body hormones are secreted from the endocrine glands. These hormones affect how we feel, think, act and the health status of our organs.

I have found working with the seven chakras a kind off miraculous experience. Imagine being able to have confidence when you speak in public, effectively getting rid of emotional garbage, increasing your magnetism, being more adventurous and innovative. Now imagine that you can do each of these by understanding the seven major chakras, their functions and the techniques to tap into their tremendous store house of power. Grasping an understanding of the chakras is not a difficult thing. When you do it is similar to discovering the master key to your personal vault that just happens to hold all your inheritance in it.

When I work with the Chakra system I assess which chakra is imbalanced through a variety of methods. Even the things your client tells you can reveal which chakra is out of balance. One client revealed that anytime they were in a difficult circumstance their throat would start hurting. As the throat chakra represents our ability to express our authentic self it became obvious that it was this chakra that was out of balance. You can hover a pendulum over each chakra. When the pendulum is telling you "yes" it swings in a clockwise direction; for "no" it goes in an anti-clockwise direction. Once you become familiar with the chakras they are a whole lot of fun to work with.

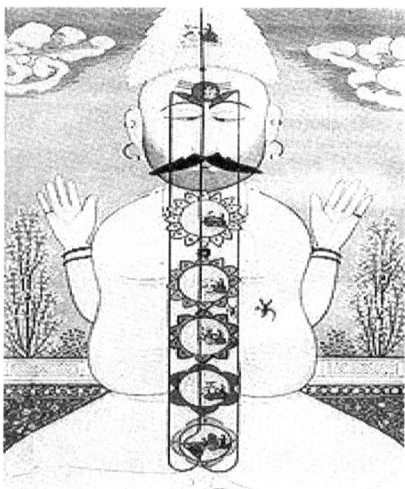

Illustration of a yogi showing the seven Chakras, Kangra school. Late 18th century A.D.

The Seven Chakras

	The crown chakra is purple/gold. It is on top the head, near the crown. It governs our higher self, knowledge and spiritual development. Connecting to spirit or God is done through this chakra. It governs the pituitary gland that controls the whole endocrine (hormone) system. The entire cerebral cortex is influenced by centre. This chakra governs physical balance and movement. Problems with this chakra can lead to a feeling of being uncoordinated, depressed and a draining feeling of being dissatisfied
	The brow chakra is dark blue. It is located between the eyebrows. This is the site of the third eye which is said to give us deep insight and intuition. It is here we gain our ability to be imaginative. This charka is connected to the pineal gland that maintains cycles of rest and activity. It is also connected to the carotid plexus of nerves. Problems with this charka can lead to a feeling of being disorientated and blocked.
	The throat chakra is light blue. It is located in the Base of the throat it rules our ability to communicate with others and our inner self. It also governs creativity. Thyroid and parathyroid glands which controls the body's metabolic rate and mineral levels. The pharyngeal plexus are found here. Problems in this area manifest as the inability to be creative and express the authentic self.
	The heart chakra is green or pink. It is in the center of the chest. It rules the heart and our ability to show true compassion and love. This chakra regulates our interaction with the outside world. It is related to the gland in the thymus, located above the heart. It is vital for growth. When this chakra is blocked feelings are withheld. Too open it leads to physical and emotional exhaustion.

	The solar plexus is yellow. It is situated below the sternum. It governs our feelings of self power and individuality. This chakra is associated with the adrenal glands and the pancreas. It is named after the complex of nerves found here and is connected to the lumbar vertebrae. A blocked or impaired chakra can lead to difficult relationships where the person feels out of control and dominated by others. The individual could also end up being the dominator.
	The sacral chakra is orange. It is located two finger widths below the navel. It governs our creativity, emotional and physical security. When we have blocked emotions it is this chakra which re-balances them. It is related to the sacral vertebrae in the spine, the sacral plexus of nerves and the sex glands. Out of balance our creativity is affected on every level and our ability to be in tune with our authentic emotions.
	The base chakra is red. It lies in the perineum, the space between the genitals and anus. When it functions properly we feel passionate, motivated, clear, grounded and confident about life. Out of balance we lack the courage and energy to live our dreams. It is related to the adrenals, testicles, ovaries and physical body.

The Seven Auras

Remember earlier it was mentioned that we radiate energy, and that is what attracts or repels people and things to or away from us? It was also said that this energy that surrounds our body is known as the aura. Each chakra in your body is associated with a particular colour which emanates in the layers of the aura. There are seven layers to the aura which penetrate each other. All the layers of the aura envelop the physical body. Each layer vibrates higher than the one before it. The layers become finer as they radiate out. The aura can be seen when you are in a meditative state. Seeing it also comes with practice.

The Holy Grail, illustration by Arthur Rackham, 1917. Pre-Raphaelite art at this time often represented contemporary interest in the "spirit body", "aura" or "body of light"

The Seven Aura Layers

1. **The etheric Body** is the nearest to the human body. As a result, it is the densest layer. When you start practicing seeing the aura, it is the layer that you see first. The colour of this aura can range from a pale gray to a bright blue. The condition of this layer reflects that of the physical body.

2. **The emotional body** is the next layer of the aura. The emotions are reflected in this layer. They appear as clouds of coloured energy within the aura. The colours change according to our emotions.

3. **The mental body** is the third layer of the aura. This layer is connected to a person's thoughts. It is mainly yellow, but you will also see the thought forms within it. The thought forms have their own colours which reflect the emotions we are experiencing.

4. **The astral layer** is the fourth layer of the aura. It is connected with love and relationships. It also forms the dividing line between the three layers, which relate to the physical world, and the three which relate to the spiritual world.

5. **The etheric** template is a blueprint of the physical body and the etheric layer. It relates to the physical body on the spiritual level. Healing is very effective at this level.

6. **The celestial body** is the sixth layer of the aura. It relates to the emotions on a spiritual level. It is here we experience unconditional love.

7. **The ketheric template** is the seventh layer of the aura. It relates to our mental processes on a spiritual level, and is where we become one with the universe.

Clearing the Chakras

When you start clearing the chakras you will experience astonishing results. I have had clients who have experienced emotional release in just one session. Once you have located your Chakra imbalance/s (remember you can have more than one) you can experience deep effective release by doing the following energy release technique. At the moment I would recommend that you just read the technique through until you get to the exercise section.

The technique is as follows:

1. Relax yourself through a few minutes of deep abdominal breathing.

2. Place your right or left hand one inch away from the chakra. Start from the base chakra working your way up to the crown chakra.

3. Ask permission to receive energy from God, Consciousness or whichever name for either you are comfortable with. Then permission to send that light to yourself.

4. Spend five minutes on each chakra and longer on those that were blocked.

5. On completion give gratitude for being allowed to direct healing energy to your body.

Once you have become use to this method add on the breathing of the appropriate chakra color. You have to spend at least five minutes on each chakra breathing in the color connected to it. So at the base chakra you imagine breathing in the energy red and allow it to circulate around the whole body; you then breathe in orange for the sacral chakra and allow that energy to energize the whole body; move onto the solar plexus and breathe in the color yellow allowing it to infuse every cell and so on.

If you have no time to do the full Energy Balancing technique it is possible to gain great benefits by concentrating on the left kidney by directing energy just below your left rib cage. It will help you to strengthen your will power, energize your body and release negative emotions. Be patient with this technique. It is really worth it for the results. For more help to discover which of your chakras is out of balance look at the simple chart below on.

Chakra Chart of Emotional Indicators

Chakra	Emotional Indicator
Crown	Not coordinated, learning difficulties, dyslexia, lack of balance, not feeling connected with spiritual self.
Brow	Thinking feels unclear, intuition and creativity feels blocked.
Throat	Inability to express inner self, problems with dry or restricted throat, blocked creativity.
Heart	Looking for love in all the wrong places, over giving, under giving.
Solar	Lack of confidence.
Sacral	Emotional issues, trauma, depression, feeling low.
Base	Not being grounded, a lack of motivation, energy and passion for life.

Sound Meditation and Healing the Story

A special note on sound meditation. It is great. I have found something interesting with sound meditation. Sometimes it happens that we are so traumatized or blocked that researching the story behind the pain is just too much. On these occasions I have discovered sound meditation is a powerful way to center and unfold ourselves. It never seems (so far, at least) to fail. Just doing ten minutes a day works wonder. Sound meditation clears all the energy centers and therefore your aura. You begin to feel clearer and more whole. Sometimes this happens after just one or two days. Buddhist say that sound meditation produces Clear Light. Meaning it clears our energy bodies so that it becomes radiant. A little bit like that dirty window analogy I used earlier. The three sounds that are very beneficial to concentrate on are the primordial sounds: Om, Ah, Hung. Each sound is produced after an inhalation and on the out breath. They are repeated one after the other. On Om concentrate on your third eye located between your eyebrows. For Ah concentrate on your throat and for Hung concentrate on your heart. There are other sounds which relate to each chakra but working with these three produces highly positive results. Om is the first primordial sound of the universe.

Crystals

Working with your chakras to heal and transform your life is even more effective when you use crystals. Crystals have been seen as sacred through the ages and have been used since time immemorial to heal the mind and body. Tutankhamen's funerary mask has a Lapis Lazuli band around his Snow Quartz and Obsidian eyes. An ancient Egyptian text states, "Lapis is the God, Amun and the god is Lapis." In 16th century Europe it was believed that the only way to cross the rivers safely or to calm a raging tempest was to carry a piece of red or white coral. This stone is seen strung over a picture of the Madonna painted by Andrea Mantegna in 1496.

Crystals are formed over millions of years from the hot molten in the core of the earth. Over a period of time a thin layer of this molten cooled and formed a thick crust which formed the earth's mantle. In this mantle new crystals continued to form as the mineral rich bubbling molten magma core boiled and moved towards the surface. It's no wonder why it is said crystals contain the DNA of the earth. At the heart of the crystal is the atom, as with all things. This atom is made up of energy particles whirling around. So the stillness of a crystal is only on the surface. It is really a whirl of vibrant energy. Another thing we should bear in mind about crystals is that they are made up of all the mineral elements that make living matter including us.

How crystals came into my life is interesting. I left London with my mum in late 2006 and headed for the Islands. We continued doing a Spa business my mum had started a few years ago. A year after our move I decided I wanted to concentrate on transformation through healing. So I left my mum's business and started my own. At the time I made the decision my husband was on his way from the United States to see me. We were newlyweds so we found ourselves living apart for a while. I could not get crystals at a good price in the Islands so on one of his visits he surprised me with a big bag of crystals which contained mostly orange carnelians and clear quartz.

It was fascinating how so many of my clients were attracted to the crystals. I think I made more money from selling crystals than from my clinics. Carnelian was the first crystal that I worked with. I found that when I used it in my healing work it made my clients feel comforted. One day I had a raging fever. My spirit moved me to place several crystals on my body. I was astounded. The fever was literally pulled out of me. Half an hour after placing the crystals on me I was completely free of my temperature. I have many more similar crystal stories to tell.

The more I have worked with crystals is the more I have come to be in awe of their amazing ability to aid in soothing and transforming our emotions. There seems to be a crystal for almost every emotional ailment. I am always amazed at the way the right crystal finds its way into your hands and life just when you need it. When working with transformation it is a good idea to choose a crystal/s to work with.

Working with Crystals

You can work with crystals in numerous ways. They work effectively in a myriad of ways: when held in your hand, under your pillow, as pendants, in gem essences, resting on the appropriate chakra point. I love creating gem essences. They allow the energy of crystals to reach many parts of your mind-body spirit system. There are many ways to create gem essences. As some gems can be toxic when placed in water, and the capacity of this book restricts me to go into all the gems into detail, I have decided it is safer to share with you a method that is completely harmless and does not require much expertise. If your curiosity is sufficiently whetted there are many great gem essence books on the market. To make your gem essence water just follow the directions below:

1. Fill a small bowl with clear spring water.
2. Decide what you want to achieve in terms of your transformation.
3. Choose from one to three relevant crystals to help you achieve the balance desired.
4. Place chosen crystals around bowl of water.
5. Leave the bowl in a quiet place for an hour.

Just a few more words about working with your gems:

1. Treat them with respect: do not throw them around or not appreciate the work they are doing for you.
2. Cleanse your gems often. This can be done by washing them in cool water, sitting them on top of salt, placing them in sunlight, sending healing light to them (refer back to working with the Energy Balancing technique). You can leave your gems to cleanse overnight.
3. When carrying your gems on you it is a good idea to carry them in a pouch. This protects their energy.

Affirmations

Sometimes we see so much about affirmations that they feel like a holistic cliché from well meaning healers and "go for it" motivators. But they do work. As we journey on bravely, affirmations can be the supporting soldiers that help us to keep on going. Imagine how many times in the day you say something negative either out aloud or to yourself. Those negative statements start forming little mountains of truth within our subconsciousness. So imagine just for one moment telling yourself the opposite of your daily pseudo truths (negative statements). So don't under estimate positive affirmations. They send loud and clear messages to our minds and cells that we want success, abundance and all the good things of life.

Affirmations are made in the present tense. So if you desire abundance you have to bear in mind that you are already tapped into an abundant flow of energy. Therefore, your affirmation is a positive statement that reflects this reality. An abundance affirmation can sound something like: "everyday I am filled with abundance", "I am abundant", "I am wealthy", "I open myself to the abundant flow of energy". While an affirmation that concentrates on love could sound something like: "I am filled with love", "I open myself to receiving love", "I am a loving beautiful person".

Crystal Table

Crystal	Chakra	Effect
Amethyst	Crown	Complete emotional balance, inner peace. Awakens perception, ability to judge, dealing with sorrow and conflict.
Fluorite	Crown and brow	Balanced emotions, order, self determination, mental and emotional flexibility, concentration, thinking, and learning.
Blue Lace Agate	Throat	Release self expression, releases anger, and harmonizes emotions.
Sodalite	Brow	Striving for truth, awareness, idealism, being true to oneself, improves group communication.
Amazonite	Heart	Self-determination, responsibility for self, inner harmony, trust, balance.
Aventurine	Heart	A carefree attitude, relaxation, inner peace, emotional regeneration, alleviates stress, pain and

skin eruptions.

Rose quartz	Heart	Love, warmth, empathy, sensitivity, romance, sexuality, balanced emotions.
Amber	Solar Plexus	Self awareness, inner freedom, happiness, cheerfulness.
Citrine	Solar Plexus	Self expression, self confidence, courage for life, dynamism, alleviates grief, strengthens immunity, nerves, digestions and internal emotions.
Gold stone	Solar Plexus	Warmth, joy, and prosperity.
Carnelian	Sacral	Courage, overcoming difficulties, willingness to help, sociability, removing inhibitions, alleviates past emotional pain.

	Moonstone	Sacral	Empathy, openness of feeling, awakens intuition, perception, helps with female reproductive issues, aids remembering of dreams, awakens feminine energy.
	Tigers eye	Base	Insight, detachment, energy, alleviates stress.
	Black Tourmaline	Base	Wards of negative influences, composure, improves sleep, creates feeling of being grounded.
	Clear quartz	All	Balanced mind, body, spirit, clears blockages.
	Mookaite	All	General healing, creativity, flexibility of thinking and emotions, releasing inner child.

How to do Forgiveness

A note on forgiveness. It is very important to aiding both physical and emotional health. Look at which illness or dis-ease within the body you are manifesting and in which part of your body. Examine the point this discomfort began to manifest itself to you. What were your feelings at the time? Being honest with yourself can be painful but will release you into healing. Now accept that you need to release the negative emotions you are holding inside in order to regain the sense of wellness you are looking for.

Releasing illness in the body can be done by Forgiveness. Forgiveness is one of the most powerful forms of release. How do you do this? Give yourself at least 7 days and each evening spend quiet time with yourself and say out loud: I forgive_____ (let a name come to you). Keep on repeating the sentence. You may discover something very interesting. You may find that many names (ones you didn't even think you remember) start coming to you. This part of your exercise may feel very emotional, and that is okay – that is the power of release at work).

Next express gratitude. Mr. Emoto found that beautiful water crystals were formed when gratitude was expressed. A family in Japan that read about his work did an interesting experiment. They put rice in two glass jars and every day for a month said "Thank you" to one jar and "You fool" to the other and then they tracked how the rice changed over the period. After a month, the rice that was told "thank you" started to ferment, with a mellow smell like that of malt, while the rice that was exposed to "you fool" rotted and turned black. After he published the results of this experiment hundreds of families from all over Japan conducted the experiment with the same results. Fascinating,, right?

The best way to express gratitude is after your forgiveness exercise and or every morning/evening. Say I give gratitude to the universe for_____. You will be sincerely surprised at the length of the list of things you are grateful for. You will also be surprised to find that over a few weeks of saying gratitude how your health begins to shift in a positive direction. Not only your physical health but the health of your projects, finances, relationships will shift positively.

To really work further and deeper with healing your illness you can prepare Hado water for drinking. Mr. Emoto suggest: (1) put water in a bottle (2) talk to the water out aloud expressing love and gratitude. So if you want A house, mention it is the present tense (I have a beautiful house, I have a beautiful body, I have a beautiful and healthy relationship). (3) Write words of gratitude and love on a piece of paper and tape it onto the bottle with the writing facing the inside. (4) Talk positive words to the water from time to time. (5) Occasionally shake the bottle to activate the water and contribute to the vibrations.

(6) Drink five glasses of this water every day. I have tried this exercise myself and it turned many aspects of my life around.

Meditation for daily balance

As part of your daily program of keeping emotional balance, it is important to incorporate a practice such as deep abdominal breathing into your daily routine. This is the key to achieving a peaceful meditative state. Meditation allows us to screen out the noise of the world and connect with our inner authentic selves and true voice. It also helps in aiding physical and emotional health. There are many people who claim they cannot meditate. This can be rectified by understanding it is the breath and not the conscious mind which aids in obtaining the meditation state. Playing music also helps to distract the left half of the brain which just loves to chatter. The technique to getting anyone to meditate is as follows:

1. Sit on a straight back chair
2. Place hands palm down on your lap
3. Ensure feet are resting on the ground
4. Sit with a straight posture, achieved by slumping in your chair and pulling yourself up by the waist
5. Breathe in slowly through your nose filling your abdomen up, one inch below your belly button.
6. Pause
7. Breathe out slowly by gently pulling your stomach in and gently allowing the air to be released.

The more you do this technique is the more natural it will become. Most of us have learned how to breathe incorrectly. This technique re-educates the body on how to breathe in a way that increases emotional and physical wellbeing.

Healing Journey Exercises

For all these exercises please create quiet time. Ensure you have created a state of deep relaxation through the meditation breath exercise detailed in this chapter. When you are sufficiently relaxed you are ready to start this part of your journey.

My Pain Comes From?

As we said you are where you are because of what has gone before you. Now is the time to discover your story. Let's look at the story behind your pain. Answer the following questions. Remember to trust your answers. The subconscious knows more than you realize. Trust it. You can repeat this exercise more than once. Each time you will receive more clarification.

- What was your relationship like with your mother?
- What was the relationship like with your father?
- What was the relationship like with your siblings?
- What were your early years like?
- What were your college years like?
- What has your adult life been like?
- Are there any patterns you have observed from your answers?
- Where do your patterns appear to originate from?

Having difficulties with locating your pain? Then do the sound meditation. It will help to clear your mind. Precede to the other steps.

Which Chakra is out of balance

Remember we said that pain is being held somewhere. Where is it for you? Ask your subconscious which chakra it is out of balance. So you may ask, "is my throat chakra in balance?" The pendulum will swing clockwise for "yes" and anti-clockwise for "no". Make sure that you write your answers down.

Releasing the Pain

Now it is time to release your pain. Follow the instructions in this chapter on the Energy Release exercise. Also use crystals, affirmations and the Forgiveness exercise.

Keeping Balance

Do the meditation breathing exercises daily. They will help to keep you balanced along with the energy release techniques.

Journey Pages

The center that I cannot find is
known to my unconscious mind.
W.H AUDEN

_____

_____

_____

_____

_____

_____

_____

_____

_____

_____

_____

_____

_____

_____

_____

_____

_____

_____

_____

_____

_____

Journey Pages

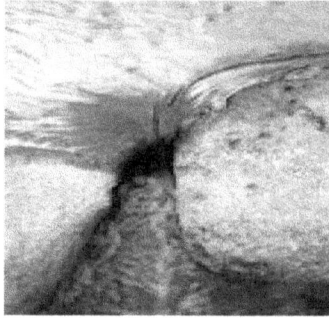

Principle 3: Awaken The Inner Eye

The more efficient a force is, the
More silent and the more subtle it is.
Mahatma Gandhi

The Dreaming

The more we heal is the more we will begin to hear that small voice of inner wisdom. The path of our recovery cannot be done without it. Our inner voice is non other than the conscious force of all knowing speaking louder to us. It has always been there. It has always guided us. The difference now to then, is that we are learning to trust and hear it more. When we trust that voice, ultimately we are trusting ourselves and knowing that we do have the answers within. When we are aching we know that something is hurting inside so it is time to stop and take a look. When we feel angry we know that someone has violated our boundaries and when we feel an urge to go somewhere we know that there is something we will get for our journey. My husband calls it "bumping heads with the other world". The aborigines and other indigenous cultures called it being in tune with Dreamtime. That is the time when all the laws of earth were laid down and held within the songs, and sacred stories as a forever reminder to us.

It is said that Daoist believed that our true intelligence and wisdom was awakened when we learned to be with nature and listen to the sea of consciousness. It was then we could recognize and sense the unity in all things. Our Western minds are so busy deconstructing everything, that we have lost the power of our sixth sense which moves us to act in accordance with the law of abundance and oneness. Tuned into it we are able to cultivate our spirituality and develop a kind character. We no longer see the world as separate but an infinite whole.

The more open we become is the more we will find ourselves guided. My advice to you is to listen to this voice very carefully. I think you will enjoy the sense of security your world begins to take on as you listen to it more.

The Dreamy Eye

I want to talk about dreams because as you heal you may find the quality of your dreams begin to change. Consciousness will talk to you through messages on cups, posters, conversations in between friends, books, and your dreams. Don't ignore these messages they can often prove to be just what you needed to know. I have had many life changing messages and visions given to me through various means, especially dreams. I come from a whole lineage of dreamers. I remember when I spent a few years in the Islands as a small child neighbors would come to my great aunts house to get their dreams interpreted.

Many cultures have recognized the power of dreams to inform and support us.

There's many an executive boss who now values the power of creative dreaming. Hippocrates saw dreams as an important way of diagnosing clients and their illness. While Sigmund Freud's *The Interpretation of Dreams* brought dreams into the era of modern psychology and psychoanalysis. Many modern day psychologists believe that lucid dreaming, when you are aware of your dreams, as being an important and valuable part of personal growth. While the ancients such as the Tibetans added a deeper dimension to this belief. For dreaming is a way we cut through the illusions of the mind and become completely one with our "dream body", our "clear essence", our deep inner selves that is part of the whole. Part of the Oneness of life.

Waking within dreams

His Holiness the Fourteenth Dalai Lama revealed that dreaming is very important to spiritual awakening and self empowerment, "there is said to be a relationship between dreaming, on the one hand, and the gross and subtle levels of the body on the other. But it is also said that there is a 'special dream state.' In that state, the special dream body is created from the mind and from vital energy (prana) within the body. This special dream body is able to dissociate entirely from the gross physical body and travel elsewhere."

There are many benefits of waking within our dreams. They include:

- Increase clarity and lucidity, both waking and sleeping
- Help us realize the transparent, dream-like nature of experience
- Free the mind
- Release energy blockages and accumulated tension and stress
- Loosen habits and make us more open, attuned, and flexible
- Unleash and mobilize creativity
- Bring repressions and denials into consciousness
- Clarify and dispel confusion
- Solve problems
- Reveal the process of death and rebirth
- Heal and relax us
- Expose fantasies
- Unlock aspirations and potentials
- Facilitate direct encounters with our shadow nature
- Provide spiritual blessings, visions, and guidance
- Help open our innate psychic capacities

- Remove hindrances and obstacles
- Help prepare (rehearse) us for death and the afterlife

Personal experience with dreams

I have had many personal experiences with dreams. I have had many dreams guide my life. In fact all of my key life events have resulted from dreams: life purpose, my life service to ecology, and much more. My family love sharing our dreams. In fact, our greeting seems to be "Are you okay this morning? Did you dream anything?"I remember there was a time when I would ignore my dreams. I think that ceased after the death of my grandmother. I dreamed I could see inside her stomach. She seemed to have a lump growing in it. I realized in the dream she had cancer. An old woman in the dream told me to go and tell my grandmother straight away. But how do you tell someone, you dreamed they have cancer. So I didn't. Six months latter it was discovered by accident that my grandmother had cancer in the stomach. A month latter she died.

It was on the discovery of her cancer I told the family my dream. For a long time I felt remorse that I had not followed the advice of my dream. I have had many more dreams of prediction, advice and guidance. So every day I check in on mine and my family's dreams.

The more you pay attention to your dreams is the more you will find your intuition opening up. You will begin to gain many ideas to improve your personal, physical, creative life and purpose. Then you find that in your day time life you have more incidences of what we sometimes see as "coincidences" happening. For many of us they feel like mini miracles.

The Four Dream States

To understand how to tap into the power of our dreams we need to know the four cycles of sleeping. They are:

- Hypnagogic sleep - the state of drowsiness we experience as we begin falling asleep
- Ordinary sleep- here, we enter a true sleeping state, but can still be easily awakened
- Deeper sleep - vital functions slow down, and we are more likely to sleep through disturbances
- Deep sleep - muscles are totally relaxed, and it would be difficult to wake us up (we only spend about fifteen percent of our sleeping hours at this stage)
- It is said that it takes about an hour to go through all four stages of sleep. Once we

have reached the fourth stage then we go back in reverse order to stage 1. Before we begin the cycle again we experience rapid eye movements (REM) under our closed lids. Research reveals that this is when we dream. We spend twenty to twenty-five percent of our sleep time in this state. This period last from a few minutes to half an hour. With practice we can enhance this stage of our sleep state allowing us to tap into the power of our dreams.

Types of dreams

Traditionally there are different types of dreams. These types of dream are mentioned in all cultures.

The texts of Tibetan dream yoga detail these dreams as being of three types: ordinary, karmic dreams, arising mostly from the activities of the day, and from our previous life activities, thoughts, experiences and personal contacts. We also have "clear light" dreams which are those containing spiritual blessings, visions and energy openings. Then there is lucid dreaming which is characterized by our awareness when we are dreaming. These three categories can be further subdivided under a further six categories. Which are said to be:

- Dreams of events that occurred while we were still awake
- Dreams about other people, alive or dead
- Forgotten elements emerging from the subconscious
- Archetypal content, evocative symbols, and so on
- Extrasensory perceptions, profound dreams, and omens
- Radiant, luminous, spiritual dreams
- Recurrent dreams, nightmares, dreams of death, and other kinds of commonly reported dreams all fall within the first four dream categories. In the interests of developing deeper awareness of your dreams, you may find it helpful to identify the category that applies whenever you recall a particular dream.

Dreamtime Practice

Meditation

Meditation actually takes us through the four cycles of sleep. The more we practice meditation, is the more moments we can experience a state of healing wakefulness. We experience a clearer state of mind, the awakening of awareness, intuition, and guidance. Start with the Basic Breath Meditation from Principle 2. I really want to emphasize something about meditation. Please, please remember you will only go into a full meditative state after about fifteen minutes of deep abdominal breathing. Do not try to focus or visualize on anything until you feel the signs of feeling heavier or lighter (indications you are entering the meditation state). Also music will help to keep the left side of your brain occupied. It is the left side that loves to chatter and talk. Eventually the music but specifically the breathing will lull it into quietness.

Daytime Dream Practice

During the day have fun and regard the world and all phenomena and experiences as dreamlike, insubstantial, and unreal. This practice actually helps us to release attachments to things. From personal experience you become less reactionary to life events and circumstances and feel surprisingly more in control. This practice also prepares the ground for much more lucid and spiritual dreaming.

Night time Practice

There is much written on how to develop your dream state. Dream practice is an ancient one and so many of the techniques are quite intense. From experience I have discovered simple is better to begin with. Try the following:

- Before bedtime do some simple yoga stretches/stretches
- Chose a crystal or stone that you feel drawn to. This you will hold in your hand while you sleep. I have found that Shuttukite is an excellent stone for dream traveling.
- When you are in bed ask permission to travel and receive information during your sleep state. Ask that you remember everything during this state.
- Do a Meditation starting from your Base Chakra and work your way up to the Crown Chakra. You will most probably find that you fall asleep by the time you get to your heart or Throat Chakra. See section on principle 2 for more information on this.
- On awaking do not speak but spend time trying to recall your dreams. Write them down in a journal. Note that if you jump out of your sleep you are more likely to forget them. If you find that you have to jump out of your sleep state. Go back into the rest state and relax. You may find fragments of your dreams come back to you.

Helping your practice

- Pay careful attention to your dreams
- Record your dreams in a dream journal upon waking each morning
- Recognize recurrent images, themes, associations, and patterns
- Contemplate the archetypal, symbolic content and meanings of your dreams
- Reflect on the similarities and differences between night dreams, daydreams, fantasies, visions, ideas, projections, and so on
- Meditate to develop the inner clarity of the Clear Light Mind - the mind unaffected by illusion
- During the day, maintain awareness that everything you experience is like a dream
- This may sound strange but I have found getting in touch with our creative side has a great effect on opening up our intuition and sensitivity. Also an instrument like the Native American flute is a powerful tool that will give you access to your heart. What I love about it you don't have to be a great musician or know how to read music. You just play from your heart. The sounds that come out are amazing!
- If you ignore the messages of your dream then it is more difficult for your inner self to keep on opening up to you through this state. The more you give them special attention is the more you get out of them.

Gaining solutions

Through your dream state you can gain deep spiritual and self awareness. You can also begin to gain answers to your conscious questions. I have discovered that if you have something you really want to know then just ask the question before going to bed saying you ask permission to receive an answer. Often you will wake-up with the solution. Sometimes the solution will come to you a few days later.

The Power of Intention

At this point it would be a good idea to talk about intention. Intention is a very powerful thing. I wish I had discovered it years ago as I struggled with my path of attainment. For years I meditated, prayed and did Yoga. Even though I helped heal the lives of many I found my own life was somewhat impoverished. Nothing ever seemed to work out for me. I was definitely a talented healer but why was my own life not experiencing major transformations, especially in the area of abundance. Then one day I woke up from my night of dreaming. "Intention. You have been missing intention". Those words hit me like a thunderbolt. For a few days I began to think on intention. I wanted to know what it really was.

Intention is clarity

I discovered that Intention is quite simply holding a clear thought and truly believing this is what you want to happen. When you have clear intention you are tapping into the energy of intention. You are connecting to the Source, Creator, Pure Awareness, and Higher Consciousness. This is the place that really makes things happen. It is the field of creative energy behind all existence. Wayne Dyer says in his book, *The Power of Intention*, it's "a force we all have within us -- a field of energy that flows invisibly beyond the reach of our normal, everyday habitual patterns." Most of us do not have clear intention. We have foggy thinking.

The Higher Way

My husband has a way of making things happen for him so I decided to ask him how does he think intention works. He explained, "You can have more than one intention but you must always make sure that your intention is aligned with your soul purpose. No sense putting out intentions that are not."

Outstanding Results

A few days after working with intention I noticed how things began to happen. Steven Pavlini author of Personal Development for Smart People has some very interesting information on his website. He mentions that within about 24 hours of putting his intention out there he starts getting validation that his intention has been heard and received. He calls this Alpha Reflection. He states after a few days of validation there is a lull "the calm before the storm'. This is the stage when most of us can give up but he says "don't" because you are in the stage of "beta reflection" which is "the rolling thunder that arrives much latter".

Pavlini was correct. Intention is powerful and it does go through various stages. There is definitely the stage of validation. It feels like many coincidences. Then there is the unmistakable stage of personal disinterest and then "bam" your intention hits you suddenly.

61

As I said within days of working with the power of intention things began to happen. I was even able to tick of one very important intention of my list within a few weeks of working with it. Intention is like a magic pill. But Pavlini was right you really have to stay with it.

Just as I was wrapping up this book, a story appeared in the news about an unemployed 50 something amateur metal detector, called Terry Herbet. Mr. Herbert discovered the largest loot of Anglo Saxon gold ever. As a result he was set to receive an award of at least of $1m. How did he find this loot? He claimed that before his regular jaunts of looking for relics from the past he would always say, "Spirits of yesteryear help me to find coins." However, the morning he found the loot of gold he changed the words "coins" to "gold". My husband joked that everyone who came across the story would surely be tempted to use the same statement.

For two days after reading the story I became one of those people my husband was talking about. I repeated the affirmation "spirits of yesteryear" statement every morning after my meditation. On the third day I went to a martial arts tournament with my husband and son. On the way back we stopped in Waxhaw, a cute North Carolinian historic town. There we discovered a lovely bead shop. One of the owners of the shop took my husband into a little corner where he had some goodies stashed behind a glass counter. After rummaging for a while he came out with a small glass tube of gold. He informed my husband the gold had been discovered in a place that was open to the public who were allowed to pan for gold. Behind the counter he also had everything that was needed for the said activity. He gave my husband directions and a leaflet so that we could find our gold. He guarantied us, gold we would definitely find. We didn't think about it any further until the following day in my meditation I heard a small audible voice say, "We sent you gold. Didn't you realize?" I couldn't stop chuckling. I was very impressed my request had been answered, but I also vowed next time I would be more specific.

Journey pages

I finally realized that being grateful was
giving more love to myself
OPRAH WINFREY

_____

_____

_____

_____

_____

_____

_____

_____

_____

_____

_____

_____

_____

_____

_____

_____

_____

_____

_____

Principle 4: Awaken Body Bliss

Shoot for the moon
Even if you miss it you will land among
the stars

LES BROWN

The Art of Seasonal Balance

As you journey into awakening your life and dreams things should appear to be much brighter. To help you make it even brighter is the art of keeping in Seasonal Balance. I first heard about this when I did my second degree in Complementary Health and Ayurvedic medicine at Middlesex University, United Kingdom. I discovered that understanding the rules to keeping my mind and body in balance for every season was crucial to a well, vibrant and happy life. It made me realize that when I spent part of my childhood in the Islands the older generation I encountered were very much into the idea of Seasonal Balance. Every change of season we were given purges and had to do a little fast. We also had certain days we had soup, certain days we had meat and fish. I know my mother who is Jamaican experienced this lifestyle even more so than I did.

However, the art and science of Seasonal Balance was learned in much more detail during my Ayurvedic degree. I loved learning about it because the principles were simple to grasp and they really worked. Based on the natural rhythms of time, energy and plain old common sense the art of Seasonal Balance will inform you to wear warm clothes in the winter, massage your feet to alleviate stress, eat light when you want to loose weight. It also informs you that imbalance does not just happen but it occurs in six stages. At each stage we are given a chance to get ourselves back into equilibrium. The six stages of imbalance are: accumulation, aggravation, dissemination, localization, manifestation and disruption of the energy states which make up our mind-body system known as doshas. These energy states in fact infuse everything in life. There are three doshas (energy states) which are each created by the combination of two fundamental primordial elements of nature: Vata likened to the wind is made up of ether and air; Pitta likened to fire is made up of fire and water; Kapha likened to Mother Earth is made up of water and earth. Vata governs all movement in the body; Pitta governs metabolism and Kapha solidity.

So when we say we feel balanced we are saying that these subtle energy states, which make us up, are in equilibrium. As we said earlier they become out of balance in a process of six stages. So what are these stages we keep on talking about? The first three stages are a state of general imbalance caused by indulging in the wrong diet, lifestyle and emotions. Here we have general symptoms of "I don't feel at my best". Ignore these messages and ignore the souls attempt to gently and quickly get you back on track. The beauty here is that simply making minor changes to our lifestyle, nutrition and emotional world will get us back to where we need to be – vibrant again.

Ignore the signs and messages then you move into the fourth stage where the subtle body energies flow into an area of weakness such as somewhere you had an old sports injury. Then you begin to feel pain in a more localized way. You may experience chronic fatigue and a general feeling of aching. You still have a chance to get it right through nutrition, lifestyle and emotional healing.

Still ignoring those signs? Then your body goes right for the fifth stage. Now you will see a flare up of an illness such as arthritis, boils etc. You better start living the philosophy of Balance and drinking those medicinal herbs before you move right on into the sixth stage where you will experience chronic illness.

Illness as a Message

As we moved through the six stages of imbalance you may have noticed I kept on mentioning "heeding the soul's message". It is important that you understand that illness is more than a disease or a mechanical thing that happens to us. Instead it is a message from our soul. I remember once waking up from a dream thinking about plants. We know when a plant is ailing because we see that it is wilting and no longer able to perform its soul function of giving its beauty and nourishment to the world. We associate the plant's illness very much with its functioning. Everything in life, including us, has functions that God has assigned to us through our soul missions. Illness is really the onset of something going wrong somewhere within us. In Ayurveda nutrition and lifestyle goes beyond eating just the right things, it goes into how you are thinking and nourishing your mind-body and soul. All of these things become important in our striving for total balance, peace and joy.

As Bernies Siegal, M.D stated in his book, *Peace, Love and Healing*, "there is always more to disease than mere physical diagnosis." He further stated, "When you ask people to describe their disease, fewer than 5 percent say things like "I have far-advanced ovarian cancer" or "carcinoma of the colon." He goes onto explain that individuals normally describe their illness in terms of "the life that gave rise to it."

I once had a dream where I was told to stop eating that dark stuff. I woke up thinking "what is the dark stuff?" I could not figure it out until the small light of enlightenment emerged from the tunnel of darkness. The "dark stuff" was none other than my favorite chocolate peanuts. "Oh no, they can't be asking me to give up my favorite chocolate peanuts. No way!" I protested out aloud to myself. I just love chocolate coated peanuts. They were my favorite treat. Okay, my skin always looked a little less than smooth afterward, but did I care?

Despite my love of chocolate coated peanuts I did heed the dream. Well, that was until my husband and I had our second Humanity4Water award ceremony in September 2009. I bought the most delicious chocolates for the ceremony. The night before the ceremony I was up late printing brochures and putting the chocolates into cute white net wedding style bags. It was just too much temptation. I just had to have one of the chocolates. It was delicious. I convinced myself I would have one more piece of chocolate. That one more turned into thirty pieces of chocolate. I was disgusted with my lack of will power. I vowed on the spot, "I will never eat chocolate again." I really knew I shouldn't.

The ceremony went really well. Afterward, we had two big bags of delicious tempting chocolate left. I put them in my cupboard and proceeded to ignore them. That was until I saw my husband have one. Once again, I convinced myself I would join him and have only one. Later that day, while my husband was not in the room I secreted up to ten more chocolates, curled up in my bed and ate them with glee over a good book. Every day I would do the same thing – eat up to ten chocolates when my husband's prying eyes were not around. In a few days all the chocolates were finished. The day after my chocolate binge I had three boils underneath my arm.

I knew my body was giving me a final warning "stop eating the junk". Once again, I vowed "I will stop eating chocolate. I will stop eating chocolate." I did stop eating chocolate but I turned my desire onto Potato Chips (crisp) and French Fries. Oh how I was enjoying my little binges until a few days later I developed a painful blister on my tongue. I had never had a blister on my tongue before. Have you ever tried to eat with a blister on your tongue? It's really painful. On one of my french-fry binges I discovered I could not eat properly. The pain on my tongue was too excruciating. My body was giving me a message again - "stop eating that junk". This time it put a blister right on my tongue so that I could not eat anything junky at all. Do you think I heeded the message of my body this time? I did. It gave me no choice.

Those faithful "messengers of the soul" will keep on nudging us until we take heed. Ignore the voice, and it will just find another way to tell you the same thing. Ignoring its messages is like trying to ignore the message your house is burning. Not a good idea. I remember helping a friend manage his bone cancer with traditional Ayurvedic nutritional principles. He started feeling much better. But on talking to him I realized he was dissatisfied with his job. He had worked in the Post Office for almost ten years but his book selves were piled high with books on law and humanitarian issues. He had a brilliant memory for law and a big open humanitarian heart. Deep down he would have loved to change jobs but fear and the need for security kept him there year after year.

Over those years he began to notice a pain in one of his legs. He kept on ignoring the pain in the same way he kept on ignoring his deep inner calling. One morning he woke up and the pain was excruciating. He decided to go to the doctors. A few days later it was announced he had bone cancer. He had no choice now but to stop. As the weeks increased he could not walk and he was rushed into intensive care. He had a few moments were the fragility of his life flashed before his eyes.

As you emotionally heal yourself you will see an improvement in your overall health. The information about Seasonal Balance will help you to further strengthen and master your life. I love the simplicity of the Seasonal Balance routine and how much better I feel when I implement its down to earth wisdom.

Seasonal Balance

There are four key seasons for the year. It is a good idea to know them and understand how the body and mind reacts to each one. Then to grasp the simple but effective seasonal regime and principles that help your mind-body and soul stay in balance.

The seasons are as follows: Winter governs the months of November to March; spring takes place between the months of March to April; summer rules May to August (late summer is between July-August); autumn governs September-October. The end of each season sees a build up of toxic energy created from our food, lifestyle, and emotions. That is why traditionally this was a time to definitely do a simple yet effective detox. In the West we still consciously associate spring with a time of renewal and detoxification.

Detox and the Seasons

Winter - November- March

Whether we live in Europe or the tropics the period between November and mid March is the time of universal winter. In the early part of this season the sky is cloudier and the sun's rays are more obstructed. The weather has a cooler breeze and the nights are longer. The heat of the body is obstructed by the cold.

It is a period which is governed by the universal energy of Kapha. As we said earlier on Kapha is composed of the water and earth element. It is the steady, stable, solid, cohesive and nurturing energy within every aspect of life and our bodies. During the season of winter its qualities are enhanced within and without us. Not paying attention to the principles of balance during this season results in the tendency of this energy to make us feel emotionally and physically heavy. We will also tend to gain weight steadily but surely. During this period there is a natural urge to consume Kapha's foods. They are heavy, oily comforting and have the pre-dominant taste of sweet, sour and salty. In small amounts these taste bestow the positive qualities of Kapha's nurturing upon us. However, in extreme we will experience a downward turn for the worse as we set the stage for the onset of Kapha illness. This universal energy governs the: stomach, pericardium, spleen, respiratory system, tongue, nose, hair, nails, and muscles. When out of balance it tends to lead to cystic acne, edema, swelling, sinus headaches, sore throats, respiratory problems, asthma, diabetes, cysts, and tumors.

Spring - March - April

Marks the end of the winter period, an over accumulation of Kapha, and the possibility of the onset of Kapha diseases if we do not engage in a detox regime aimed at re-balancing this universal energy again.

Summer: Early Summer (May To June)

During the period of early summer the suns rays become powerful day by day. The air becomes dry. All the moisture in the earth dries up during this season taking away the cold from the earth. It is a period where the energy of Vata predominates. Vata is the universal and bio energy in the body which governs all voluntary, involuntary movement and mental functions.

It is because of the Vata energy which represents the air and space element that we are able to experience movement of thought, intellect, spirituality, intuition and creativity through time and space. Vata has a cool, drying, light, bitter, astringent and pungent quality. Indulging in foods and activities of this nature throws this energy out of balance during this season. It is important to note that eating and over indulging in food and activities with a Vata nature will throw this energy out of balance during any season.

Out of balance Vata affects the areas that it governs such as the colon, skin, bladder, kidney, and large intestine. The diseases which manifest with a Vata imbalance include: excessive dryness, psoriasis, dandruff, wrinkles, constipation, sharp pain, backache, arthritis, nervous disorders, headaches, and insomnia.

Late Summer (July To August)

Early summer goes into late summer (Monsoon). The energy of Pitta begins to rise. This energy is related to the fire element that exists within all of life including our bodies. It governs everything to do with metabolism and is hot, pungent, drying. As this energy rises during the period of late summer the body can become debilitated and the metabolism becomes weaker. It is a time when great disease can manifest. However, this season has its upside too. Governed by the dynamism and fiery energy of Pitta the world suddenly becomes ablaze in a swirl of activity. We feel more inclined to be like Pitta - adventurous dare devils. This is a season where we want to do more and explore more.

It is also a period that sees the coming and advent of the Summer Solstice. The Summer Solstice happens towards the end of June. The word Solstice originates from the Latin word Sistit which means to stand still. It is an astronomical event that occurs twice each year, when the tilt of the Earth's axis is most inclined toward or away from the Sun, causing the Sun's apparent position in the sky to reach its northernmost or southernmost extreme. At the solstice, the Sun stands still in declination; that is, the apparent movement of the Sun's path north or south comes to a stop before reversing direction. The solstice is marked by the winter solstice and the summer solstice. During the summer solstice we experience the longest day of the year.

This is a highly spiritual time of the year and is marked by many festivals all over the world. In Nigeria leading up to the summer solstice there is the great *Festival of The Oracle* also known as The Festival of Ifa. It is a time that is marked by much national activity, which culminates in all the traditional priest, indigenous people and tourists from all over the world coming together to discover what message the ancient oracle carries for the year. This time is seen as the real beginning of the year amongst the Yoruba and around the world. In England over 19000 people gather at the famous sacred site of Stonehenge to celebrate the summer solstice.

End of Summer

At the end of the whole summer period Vata, the universal energy associated with the air and space element, has become over accumulated. It's over accumulation may have been further escalated by over indulging in foods and activates that contain its cool, drying, light, mobile (too much rushing and movement), astringent, pungent, bitter qualities. Without putting in a plan of action to re-balance this energy through detoxification you are sure to begin to suffer from the Vata illness mentioned earlier in this chapter.

Autumn. September to October

In this season the sun moves towards the South. It is a time when the earth is beginning to cool down. Ancient Ayurvedic text says it is a time to enjoy moonlight strolls and moonlight chats. This is a time when we should stay away from excessive indulgence of food and activities with a Pitta quality: hot, sharp, slightly oily, sour, light, fluid, pungent, sweet, and salty. By the end of this season Pitta has naturally accumulated. If a healthy regime has not been observed its build up will be excessive. Governing the following organs: liver, gall bladder, small intestine and heart - an over build up of the Pitta bio energy will cause the following diseases: acne, rosacea, rashes, cold sores, allergic, reactions, burning sensations, peptic ulcers, bleeding disorders, hypertension and falling hair.

Detoxification

Detoxification does not mean to starve oneself but to give the body a chance to return back to a state of balance by removing toxins. It is the same as fasting. There are many different types of fast, but in essence fasting is to withdraw from our 'normal" pattern of eating and lifestyle for a set number of days. The aim - to remove the build up of toxins within the system. Traditionally, toxins are the excessive build up of our universal energies (dosha) which are responsible for the functionality of life itself. Toxins are also seen as food that is partially digested as a result of an improper diet and lifestyle which gives rise to digestive malfunctioning.

The ancients saw the process of detoxification as "lightening up". Just one day of this process can make us feel lighter, more energized, creative, and ready to go for life. The therapeutic process of "lightening up" includes sweating therapies (swedena). These include: steam baths, therapeutic baths, self massage or administered massage, mud/seaweed wraps, exercise (varying from yoga, walking, light aerobics), foot baths, and a diet that helps to improve our digestive powers.

When To Detox

Traditionally the time to cleanse and re-balance our bodies and minds are: at the end of each seasonal cycle, moving from one country to another either permanently or just for holiday, when we are ill, when we are recovering from illness, when we have over indulged, when we are making a move from one life experience to another, when we are in recovery from emotional trauma or stagnation.

How many days should we detox? That depends on how severe the feeling of being out of balance is. The general rule of thumb you can apply is when: you feel tired, bloated, irritable, or lack focus a minimum of a three day detox is good. If you have merely over indulged for a day or two or just want to get back on track a one day detox goes a long way too. If you have any medical conditions ask your doctor for advice before you go on a detox.

Symptoms of Detoxing

You may experience hunger pangs, fatigue and tiredness when you do a detox. This is normal as the body is clearing itself of years of gunk. The good thing is, after wards you will feel great. Ensure you drink plenty of water during your detox. It is also important that you do it at a time when you will not be rushing around with a busy work schedule.

Detoxing is a perfect time to take quiet time for yourself and to renew your spirits. It is also a good thing to do while you go through your healing journey. As we "lighten up" through detox we begin to have a greater sense of self awareness. We can feel our pores and we begin to sense our consciousness fully through the eyes of our body and cells again.

A Japanese Study On Fasting

In a recent Japanese study on fasting we can see the great benefits that doing a detox brings. It showed that fasting therapy proved 87% effective in curing or ameliorating a wide variety of psychosomatic and mental diseases. The study, conducted by Haruyosi Yamamoto, Jinichi Suzuki and Yuichi Yamauchi of the Department of Psychosomatic Medicine, Nagamachi Branch Hospital, Tohoku University School of Medicine, Sendai, Japan, involved 380 patients who underwent a complete fast for 10 days.

Throughout the fasting period, patients lived in an ashram-like atmosphere conducive to self-analysis and relaxation, and free from the usual distractions of daily life. Patients were accommodated in private rooms, but newspapers, radio and television were prohibited, as well as all non-medical visitors. In this way experimenters preserved the optimal conditions for mental introspection, enhanced self-awareness and physical purification which enabled the patients to successfully recognize and come to grips with their problems without outside distractions or interference.

During the course of therapy, patients were encouraged to drink a minimum of 1000 mils. (10 glasses) of water per day to maintain tissue hydration and to promote internal cleansing and elimination of wastes from the body tissues. In addition, 500 mils. of 5% pentose solution, containing various vitamins and small amounts of essential amino acids, was administered intravenously every day. This provides the body with a minimal level of nutrition, without activating the digestive process. It thus allows the self-purification of the fasting process to proceed unimpeded for the 10 day period, without placing excessive demands on patients unfamiliar with fasting prior to the experiment.

Return to normal diet was strictly supervised over 5 days after the conclusion of the 10 day fasting period, to ensure that metabolic and physiological re-adaption to a normal diet and lifestyle occurred without mishap. The return to normal diet followed the order of fluid diet, soft diet, then ordinary Japanese style diet.

Meditation And Relaxation

In order to encourage relaxation and to enhance introspection and self-analysis, a method of meditative reflection known in Japanese as naikan was practiced on various occasions. This practice is similar to the process of antar mouna, where one learns to objectively witness the flow of thoughts, feelings and experiences without identifying with them.

In addition, patients learned the practice of yoga nidra, which has been introduced into medical circles as the system of autogenic relaxation training. This enabled the patients to relax the body, mind and emotions deeply and systematically at various times throughout the day, entering the state of yoga nidra (psychic sleep) according to their needs and inclinations.

The results

The 380 patients involved were suffering from a wide variety of psychosomatic diseases and mental disorders at the outset of the experiment. Most had undergone prior medical treatment for several months or years for management of their symptoms. At the time of discharge, their clinical conditions were reassessed. This revealed an outstanding overall efficacy rate of 87% for fasting therapy.

Researchers reported a 24% rating of 'excellent', signifying the disappearance of all symptoms or cure of the disease, a 63% rating of "good' and a 13% rating of 'ineffective'.

A Friend Called Sleep

I would like to give a special mention to the subject of sleep. It is crucial part of keeping mind-body and soul balance. Let's admit it, when we do not get enough sleep we are ratty, irritable, spaced out and groggy. Research has shown what we already know – getting enough rest and sleep is crucial. In a 2002 poll, over 80% of American adults believed that not getting enough sleep leads to poor performance at work, risk of injury, poor health and difficulty getting on with others. Recent research also indicates that sleeping impacts on aging and diabetes.

So what do we need to know about sleep? Well, it is regulated by two brain processes. One is the restorative process; the other the process that controls the timing of sleep. The first kicks in according to how many waking hours we have. The more hours we have had awake the stronger the urge to sleep is. The second process helps us to feel sleepy during the night time and awake in the day. It is governed by the circadian biological clock that is located in the part of the brain known as SCN (Suprachiasmatic nucleus). The SCN is influenced by light so that we naturally tend to get sleepy at night when it is dark and are active during the day when it is light. The circadian clock also regulates day-night cycles of most body functions ensuring that the right levels of body functioning occur at night when we are sleeping. The hormones are secreted, blood pressure is lowered and the kidney function changed. Research also indicates that memory is consolidated during sleep. It is said that establishing a regular bed and wake time helps promote sleep by getting us in sync with our circadian clock so that we experience all the stages of sleep.

Getting enough sleep most definitely impacts on the quality of our lives. We perform better the following day, we feel less sleepy during the day time, and we experience a greater sense of overall wellness. By the way, day sleeping promotes obesity. In Ayurveda sleep is known as "nidra" and getting enough of it is said to promote: happiness, nourishment, strength, sexual potency, knowledge and longevity.

In Ayurvedic medical text it is further stated that keeping very late night times promotes increased Vata and all that goes with it: excessive dryness of the skin, internal organs, and a feeling of living on our nerves. On the other hand day time sleeping increases the heavy earth energy of Kapha causing a feeling of heaviness, lethargy in the body, and weight gain. Traditionally day sleep is said to be only beneficial when one is: exhausted by heat, excess speech, walking for long distances, sexual activities, anger, grief and fear. It is also good for those who are aged, young, debilitated, wounded, suffering from indigestion or habituated through work routine to sleeping during the day.

So what is enough sleep? This varies from person to person but 7-9 hours of sleep time leaves our souls feeling restored. To promote good quality sleep:

- Avoid caffeine, nicotine close to bedtime
- Avoid alcohol
- Exercise regularly but do gentle exercises in the evening as the body is naturally winding down
- Have a healthy balanced diet and lifestyle
- Create a sleep conducive environment that is dark, quiet, cool and comfortable

Sometimes getting the right amount of sleep feels like the hardest thing but it is important to ensure you do.

Self Massage

Wherever, and whenever I can I try to demonstrate the Ayurvedic self massage (also known as Indian self massage) to friends, family members and clients. It is fantastic! I have seen legs slimmed down, nerves calmed, and dull skin lit up almost instantly. What I love is that it is so simple and it's free. It only takes a little bit of effort on your part, a little bit of oil and voila you are on your way to mind-body heaven.

Traditionally, Indian Self Massage dates back to southern India, at about 1500 BC. It is part of what is called Marma massage. Masters of kalari, an ancient Indian martial art, first discovered the power of marma points. In battle, kalari fighters targeted an opponent's marma points as a way to inflict pain and injury. According to kalari lore, people have 12 marma points that, when hit with a knockout blow, can cause instant death. These areas were so important that soldiers even used armor to protect their horses' marma points while riding into battle. Along with their ability to kill, however, comes an ability to heal.

I learned Indian Marma massage and self massage under the tutorship of Dr. Palitha and Dr. Athique. They were the two brilliant directors of the degree course in Ayurvedic medicine that I undertook at Middlesex University in the United Kingdom. Traditionally it is pointed out that massage therapy: preserves the body's energy; improves the blood circulation; skin tone and texture; helps in excreting toxins out of the body through sweat, urine and mucous; increases joy and happiness.

Traditionally massage was and is still used to aid the healing of treatment of skin disorders like eczema, blisters, scabies, seborrhea and other conditions like neurasthenia, headaches, sleeplessness, gouty arthritis, polio, obesity and mental disorders. It also increases physical stamina and mental alertness. Now that I have whetted your appetite, I am sure you want to know how to do this wonderful massage technique. Just follow the instructions below.

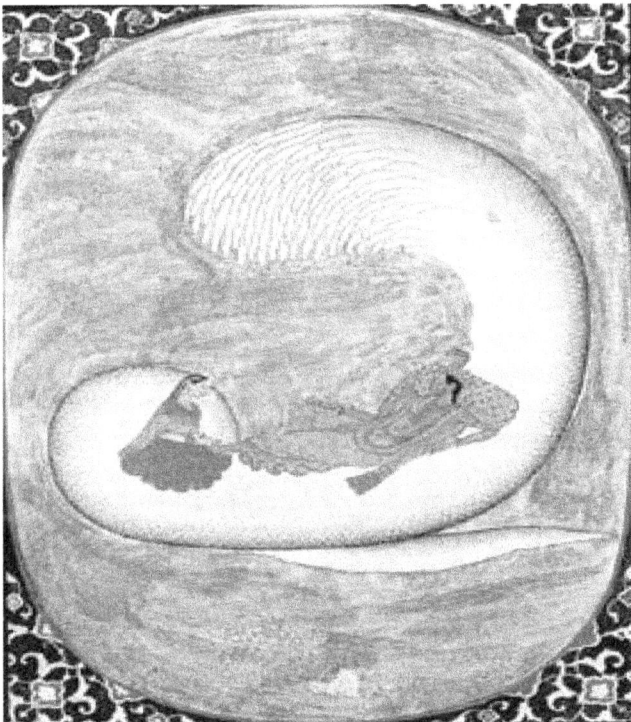

Old Indian painting of Goddess Laksmi massaging the God's Vishnu's feet.

Self Massage Technique

1. Wear a swim suit/swimming pants (ladies you can wear a sarong around you; men a towel.)
2. Stand with your legs at shoulder width.
3. Put a little base oil such as: sunflower, almond, olive oil in your hand. With this you will lubricate the part of the body you are about to work on.
4. Begin the massage by starting with your arms. Imagine there are five imaginary lines running down them. The lines start on the inside part of your arm and move outwards. Using small rotational movements begin to follow your imaginary lines in a downward movement. Start from the inside line and work your way out.
5. Now its time to move onto your waist. Once again, imagine five imaginary lines. This time follow them in upward strokes. Start from your hips and end under your arm pit.
6. Move to your legs. Your imaginary lines are now on the front and back of your legs. Starting with the front of your leg follow those imaginary lines from the inside to the outer edge of your leg. Now do the same for the back of your legs.
7. Now you are going to massage your feet. Sit on a comfortable chair/floor to do so. Your imaginary lines are now on your feet. You will follow them starting from the heel and outside part of your foot working your way inward and down to your toes.
8. Spend five minutes on each body part.
9. Dab of any excess oil with a piece of kitchen towel.

Old Papyrus showing Egyptian massage

Energy Exercise

Like massage, exercises such as Yoga and Tai Chi help us to awaken our Chi (energy), keep it moving, and prevent it from stagnation. Ultimately they awaken our connection to our inner core and the universe. Yoga, itself dates back to thousands of years and is documented within the Yoga Sutra written by sage Patanjali. The West loves to popularize things and in the process the depth of meaning gets lost in translation. Therefore it is no wonder why so many think of Yoga as merely physical exercise but it is so much more than that. There are eight petals of this ancient tradition: ethical discipline (yama), internal ethical observances (niyama), poses (asana), breath control (pranayama), sensory control and withdrawal (pratyahara), concentration (dharma), meditation (dhyana), and blissful absorption (samadhi). These petals awaken us like a beautiful flower.

In yoga, the body is seen as being made up of different layers of energy sheaths. There are five in all. The aim of life and self development is to integrate these sheaths to bring into being a sense of wholeness. The body is our outer most sheath which manifest as physical form. The others are: the energetic body, mental body, intellectual body and the soul body. It is the physical body which encompasses all the other sheaths. The sheaths are not as delineated as we have made it sound. Each one is part of the other. There must be full integration from the soul to the outer physical body and from the physical body back to the soul. In this way we are fully functional in life and infused with consciousness in all that we do.

In terms of the physical movement of Yoga or any energy system like yoga it is with the integration of all sheaths of the body and in mind, that one stretches. We allow ourselves to not only be active in life but "consciously active." As Yoga master B.KS Iyengar succinctly states in his book *Light on Life.* The Sun Salutation is a morning routine which allows us to achieve the integration and balance we strive for. It is a series of yoga poses performed in a graceful flow linked by breath.

Sun Salutation Technique

You Will Need

- Comfortable clothing suitable for stretching and moving
- A calm place where you won't be distracted or disturbed
- A yoga mat or folded blanket

Step 1.Mountain Pose: Stand at the front of your mat in the Mountain Pose, with your feet hip-width apart and your weight evenly distributed between them, your spine erect, and your arms at your sides.

Step 2. Arms Reaching Upward: Inhale into the Arms Reaching Upward Pose, extending your arms overhead, bringing your palms together, and expanding your chest.

Step 3. Standing Forward Bend: Exhale into the Standing Forward Bend, bringing your chest toward your thighs and your hands toward the floor.

Step 4. Lung Pose: Inhale into the Lunge Pose, placing your hands on the mat on either side of your right foot as you lunge your left leg straight back behind you. Expand your chest as you lengthen your spine.

Step 5: Plank Pose: Exhale into the Plank Pose, stepping your right leg back so your feet are now side by side. Look straight at the floor, keeping your arms extended and your body straight. Hold this pose for 3 to 5 full breaths.

Step 6. Kneel & lower head. Exhale, slowly dropping your knees to the floor. Untuck your toes, bring your hips back to your heels, and lower your head to the floor with your arms still extended in front of you.

Step 7. Get on all fours: Inhale, slowly bringing yourself up on all fours.

Step 8. Lower chest & chin: Exhale, slowly bending your elbows and lowering your chest and chin to the floor so your hands, knees, and feet are touching the mat.

Step 9. Upward Facing Dog: Inhale into the Upward Facing Dog Pose, pushing your head and ribcage up off the mat by fully extending your arms as you press the tops of your feet into the ground. Your thighs and hips should rise a few inches above the mat.

Step 10. Downward Facing: Do exhale into the Downward Facing Dog Pose, tucking your toes and lifting your hips up and back so that you're bearing your weight on the balls of your feet. This should create an upside-down V shape with your body. Relax your neck and allow the weight of your head to lengthen your spine.

Step 11. Lung Pose: Inhale into the Lung Pose again, stepping your left foot forward.

Step 12. Standing Forward Bend: Exhale into the Standing Forward Bend again, stepping your right foot forward next to your left foot so your weight is on both feet.

Step 13. Arms Reaching Upward: Inhale into the Arms Reaching Upward Pose again.

Step 14. Mountain Pose: Exhale, completing the Sun Salutation by returning to the Mountain Pose.

Seasonal Routine Chart

This seasonal routine chart will help you to know when to detox, balance, and renew yourself.

Season	Governing bio-energy	Governing energy	Detox-
Winter (Nov-Mar)	Kapha	Conserving energy. Time to reconcile, thoughts, energy and health.	Balancing routine
Spring Mar-April	Kapha	Time of Renewal over build up of Kapha energy.	Spring detox.
Summer early May To June	Vata	Time of creativity and dynamic movement.	Balancing routine
Summer late July – Aug	Pitta	Time of Dynamic energy.	Balancing routine
End of Summer August	Vata Pitta	Overbuild up of Vata energy. Time of the earth cooling down and getting ready for winter.	Summer detox Balancing routine
Autumn Sept-Oct	Pitta	Over accumulation of Pitta energy	Autumn detox

Kapha Seasonal Balancing Routine Chart

Dosha	Activity	Details
Kapha Mother Earth Winter Detox & Balance	Massage	Head or self massage with light almond oil or no oil at all.
	Aroma oils (bath, massage, oil burner)	Ylang Ylang, Lemongrass
	colours (wear, general use)	Incorporate rich colours such as purple and gold.
	Lifestyle	Socializing is a must to help keep this heavy slow energy in balance.
	Diet	Eliminate: refined carbohydrates, junk and over refined foods. Reduce: foods that are heavy, sweet, salty, oily cold foods and beverages such as sweets, pizza, cheese, dairy etc Avoid: over eating. It slows down the digestive system creating a build up of toxins. Incorporate: Plenty of fresh fruit and vegetables, warm beverages, foods with light, astringent and bitter taste and quality.
	Exercise	vigorous and warming – running, aerobics etc
	Affirmation	I embrace change.

Vata Seasonal Balancing Routine Chart

Dosha	Activity	Details
Vata	Massage	Head massage, self massage, self foot massage with slightly warm oil of almond, olive, castor or sesame.
Summer detox & Balance	Aroma oils (bath, massage, oil burner)	Warming basil, cedar wood, , cinnamon, dove, geranium, jasmine, juniper, lavender, myrrh, musk, orange, rose, sage and spices.
	Colours (wear, general use)	Incorporate warm colours such as red, yellow, and orange.
	Lifestyle	Slow down. Include meditation in your daily routine. Vata is aggravated by too much rushing about, and anxiety.
	Diet	Eliminate: refined carbohydrates, junk and over refined foods. Reduce: foods that are cold, dry, bitter, astringent, pungent, over light such as, oily cold foods and beverages such as potato chips (crisp) and ice cream. Avoid: erratic eating it creates a chaotic digestive system resulting in partially digested food and toxins. . Incorporate: Plenty of fresh fruit and vegetables, warm beverages, foods that are rich and nourishing such as vegetable soups.
	Exercise	Gentle and warming such as yoga, swimming, tai chi, etc
	Affirmation	I embrace the flow of life.

Pitta Seasonal Balance Chart

Dosha	Activity	Details
PITTA **Fire** **Autumn Detox &** **Balance**	Massage	Head massage, self massage, foot massage with cooling oils of almond, coconut
	Aroma oils (bath, massage, oil burner)	Cooling chamomile, cinnamon, gardenia, honeysuckle, jasmine, lavender, lotus, mint, rose, saffron and sandalwood
	Colours (wear, general use)	Incorporate cool colours such as blue, green, and white.
	Lifestyle	Slow down. Try daily meditation. Sound meditation would be good for focusing and calming your mind.
	Diet	Eliminate: refined carbohydrates, junk and over refined foods. Reduce: hot, pungent, salty, sour, such as curries or overly spicy foods. Avoid: eating too quickly and missing meals as this results in a malfunctioning digestive system. Incorporate: Plenty of fresh fruit and vegetables, cool beverages.
	Exercise	Try gentle exercises such as yoga, swimming, tai chi, etc
	Affirmation	I trust life.

1-3 detox plan

Nighttime	Purge	Night before do a castor oil purge. Follow the directions on the bottle. A good tip is to mix the recommended amounts of castor oil in orange juice. If you don't you will understand why this suggestion! If the purge doesn't work increase the dosage by one tablespoon.
Day 1 (Repeat for day 2&3)		
Morning	Exercise	Gentle stretching such as yoga, Pilates etc
	Massage Therapy	Self massage with oils chosen from seasonal energy chart.
	Bath Therapy	2 cups of Epsom salt and 3 cups of sea salt with combination of essential oils from Seasonal Energy chart.
	Meal:	Trikatu tea: 1 tablespoon of fresh ginger, pinch of cayenne, pinch of black pepper, honey to taste. Fresh Juice.
Lunch	Exercise	Gentle stretching such as yoga, Pilates etc Meal: ginger tea.
	Meal:	Trikatu tea.
Evening	Exercise	Gentle stretching such as yoga, Pilates etc
	Meal	Trikatu tea. Fresh Juice.
	Massage Therapy	Self massage with oils chosen from seasonal energy chart.
	Bath Therapy	Repeat Bath Therapy from morning.

Juicing

A note on the fresh juice for your detox. I have found that the Carrot Chaser is the juice I tend to use for most clients. It is easy to make, affordable and is packed with minerals and vitamins. It can be made thin or thickened and spiced up with coconut milk, honey and cinnamon for a more filling juice.

Carrot Chaser Basic

Juice:
4-5 carrots
1-2 apples
½ beet root
1 tablespoon of ginger
pinch of cayenne pepper
dilute with water

Caribbean Tropical Carrot Chaser

Juice:
4-5 carrots
1-2 apples
½ beet root
1 tablespoon of ginger pinch of cayenne pepper
mix coconut milk and honey to taste

Tropical Green power Chaser

Juice:

4-5 carrots
1-2 apples
½ beet root
½ bunch of spinach
½ cucumbers
1 tablespoon of ginger pinch of cayenne pepper
mix coconut milk and honey to taste

1 tablespoon blue green algae/chlorophyll powder

Tips for Juicing

- Try to buy organic fruit or veg
- Before juicing wash fruit and veg thoroughly
- Pre-chop fruit and veg. Bag in a sandwich bag and stick in the fridge. This pre-prep saves on a lot of time
- Always water juice down with choice from the following: coconut milk, coconut water, water, rice milk, soy milk or almond milk. (Try various ones for different taste)
- Juice should be drank within half an hour of juicing. However, if you want to preserve the juice turn it into a shake by adding honey and non dairy milk
- Add ginger to juice for a kick and to fire up the digestive system
- Adding chlorophyll/blue green algae or wheat germ to juice gives it that extra green power most of us need.
- Grating nutmeg into juice also gives it a wonderful taste
- DON'T BE SCARED TO EXPERIMENT!

Journey pages

*I am here for a purpose and that is to grow into a mountain,
not to shrink to a grain of sand. Henceforth I will apply all
my efforts to become the highest mountain of all.
I will strain my potential until it cries for mercy.*

OG MANDINO

Principle 5: Awaken Body Nourishment

*Saying no can
be the ultimate
self-care*

CLAUDIA BLACK

Nourishment Is?

After we detox it is important to know how to keep the bliss going as we continue our journeying into strengthening and building our physical and spiritual muscles for life. This is where the knowing the simple principles of nourishment come in handy. Once I asked workshop members, "what is nutrition?". The answers were as varied as they were fascinating. Some people said, "Nutrition is eating the right vitamins". Others said, "Nutrition is making sure I eat so I don't feel tired". There were also those who drew a blank. All of these answers were right in their own way, but what really struck me was that very few of us understand the basic principles behind nutrition. Nutrition is simple – it is the means by which we ensure total mind, body and yes spiritual nourishment. It truly is the total nourishment of the whole of who we are.

The Simple Cycle of Nutrition

I have found that by teaching people *The Simple Cycle of Nutrition* all the information about carbohydrates, vitamins, minerals, essential amino acids etc just clicks into place. Suddenly the parts become a whole and make sense.

    The Simple Cycle of Nutrition involves knowing that our beautiful bodies are made up of 60 trillion cells. Each of these cells form together to make our tissues which in term forms our organs.

    In *The Simple Cycle of Nutrition* the body must nourish our seven principle tissues: plasma, blood, fat, muscle, bone, bone marrow, egg/sperm. These tissues are fed from food essence formed in the stomach. Our food essence is made up of the food we have ingested through our mouths. If the food essence is good the tissues fed are well fed and nourished. On the other hand, if the food essence is not good (filled with partially digested food matter known as toxins) the opposite is true. If the food essence our tissues receive is "bad" then the result equals blocked elimination channels, malnourishment of cells, tissues, and organs – leading to disease.

    In *The Simple Cycle of Nutrition* it is not only what we take into our body which is crucial to the good formation of nourishing food essence but how we take those things into our bodies. So eating fast leads to undigested food matter and therefore "bad" food essence. Eating after 6pm (especially heavy meals) leads to undigested food matter and "bad" food matter.

    Understanding *The Simple Cycle of Nutrition* is easy and can revolutionize how think about ourselves and our bodies.

Creating the right food essence

Do not Over Eat

Overeating is one of the major causes of disease both mild and severe in the body. Our digestion is a delicate chemical balance. Anything that upsets that causes food to be partially digested resulting in the formation of toxic food essence. As you read earlier, when the food essence of the body is toxic then it: creates illness in vulnerable parts of the body, causes malnourishment of cellular tissue and blocked elimination channels. The result is not nice.

Ayurveda states that overeating causes Mandagni (slowed and impaired digestion). In the Vedic medical Charaka Samita it is said that the "Correct quantity of food increases life span". Our innate body intelligence lets us know this anyway. I know when I over eat I feel awful. I am sure there are few people that could claim to feel vital, alive and ready to go for it after over filling their stomachs. I saw an interesting article recently on an 8 year old British boy who weighed 218lbs. He was so overweight that British social workers wanted to take the boy into protected custody "for his own protection." His mother who appeared to be quite slim herself gave away the secret to his size "he eats double or triple what a normal eight year old would". So do Sumo Wrestlers.

But how much is too much? In reality food quantity is different for every individual. But I believe we all know when we have overeaten. For those of us who want to be doubly sure, Ayurveda reveals we should visualize the stomach and divide it into three imaginary compartments. We should fill one with foods like rice. The second with liquids like water, soup, juices. The third kept empty for air or gases. Or just make sure your meal fits in the cup of your hands. Further indicators of overeating are: obstruction in the heart, pain in sides, and heaviness in abdomen. When you have overeaten it is also uncomfortable to lie, sit, breath, laugh or talk. You will also feel as though there is a loss of strength.

Do not Under eat

Many books mention the problems about overeating, but it is also important that we do not under eat. Over eating means that we are over nourishing ourselves and when we under eat we do the opposite. Under eating provides the body with: no satisfaction of hunger and thirst, there is loss of strength, loss of immunity, damage to mental functions and damage to sense organs. It is important that our body receives the nutrients it requires for a sense of total wellness.

Do not eat too soon after meals

Eating meals too close together causes food to be only partially digested and leads to fermentation in the intestinal track. There should be four hours, at least, between each meal.

Eat a balanced food plate

The statistics vary slightly as to what a balanced food plate looks like but if you aim for 40% healthy carbohydrates, 40 % healthy protein, and 20% wholesome fat you should be on the right track.

Do not eat raw foods

The west has taken very much to the idea that raw food is best. However, the ancient Indian medical system says that raw food can hamper the digestive power. The reality is that for most of us our digestive power is very weak. Lightly steamed food or liquid drinks are a good way to still eat nutrient rich food.

Eat food at body temperature

Overly hot or overly cold food does one thing – stagnates the digestive fire. Impairment of the digestive system leads to undigested food matter (toxins) which float around the system creating disease.

Know your own body clock. Eat accordingly

Have you noticed the sun rises and sets at a certain time each day? When I lived in the Islands I became even more sensitized to this fact. The sun would rise brilliantly every morning and set brilliantly every evening. The rhythms of nature are reflected within our own bodies.

From 6-10am our body is sleepy, heavy and waking up to the world. This fact stretches to our digestive system. Between 10 am and 2pm the body is feeling more dynamic especially as it passes 12am. Our digestive system is also more fired up along with our brain power and ability to do. Between 2pm and 6pm the body is beginning to slow down and go into rest mode. The closer it gets to 6pm is the more restful it starts to become. This is the period when the digestive system and the mind begin to feel more sluggish. Between 6pm and 10pm the body is now at rest, the digestive system has more or less closed for the night. The latter will not digest anything to heavy. Between 10pm and 2am the body begins the process of assimilation of our thoughts, day and food matter. Once we reach 2am to 6am the body is involved in creative thinking, visions and dreams. It is definitely not thinking about digesting our even assimilating food but more moving things to where they need to be. At 6am this cycle begins all over again.

So what happens if you go against your natural body clock? Well imagine eating a heavy meal after 6pm. From what has been said you know the body is no longer digesting anything (particularly heavy food matter). This should tell us that what is eaten after this time remains undigested in the stomach. The result - body toxicity and weight gain. Also eating a heavy meal between 6pm to 10pm slows down the digestion, diminishes the digestive power, and causes fermentation and formation of toxins in the stomach and thus body.

Understanding and working with the body clock is one of the major secrets to good health and weight loss.

Eat food that has been properly combined

Ayurveda has much to say about food combining. It is said that food combining should be done with the utmost of care, as bad food combining can cause bad health through impairment of the digestive system.

It is said two or more food items of similar quality should not be combined. So milk has a sweet quality and sugar is sweet so these two are hazardous to mix. Milk and fish should never combine. Milk and fruit is another combination sure to cause putrefaction in the system. So all that advice about putting a banana with breakfast cereal is a disastrous idea.

The ancient principle of food combining was brought to further light by what became a popular diet – The Hay Diet by Dr. William Howard Hay. Dr. Hay introduced food combining in 1911. His basic premise was that there is one underlying cause for health problems and that is the wrong chemical condition in the body which is acidity.

This acid condition results in a lowering of the body's vital alkaline reserve, the depletion of which causes toxemia or auto intoxication (basically internal poisoning).

Dr. Hay classified foods into three types according to their chemical requirements for efficient digestion and their digestive by product. These were: -
1. Fruits and vegetables: Alkali forming as final end product in the stomach. Note even acid tasting fruits such as lemons yield alkaline salts in the body.
2. Concentrated proteins such as meat, game, fish, eggs or cheese. These foods are acid forming in their final end products in the body.
3. Concentrated carbohydrates or starch foods, which are acid forming. These include grains, bread, and all foods containing flour, all sugars and foods containing sugars (sucrose), but not the naturally occurring sugars found in fruit.

Dr. Hay's rules for food combining which reflects ancient principles of good food combining are:

1. Starches and sugars should not be eaten with proteins and acid fruits at the same meal.
2. Vegetables, salads and fruits (whether acid or sweet) if correctly combined should form the major part of the diet.
3. Proteins, starches and fats should be eaten in small quantities.
4. Only whole grains and unprocessed starches should be used and all refined and processed foods should be eliminated from the diet.
5. Not less than four hours between starch and protein meals.
6. Milk does not combine well with food and should be kept to a minimum.
7. Don't mix foods that fight. So proteins can be mixed with neutral (alkaline foods), proteins and starches should never be mixed together, starches and neutral (alkaline) foods can be mixed.

Eat food that has been prepared right

Over frying, barbecuing, and microwaving food kills the nutritional value of food. Barbecuing is known to produce carcinogenic. If you have to fry it is better to quickly stir fry in a wok. It is really better to steam food where possible and not to overcook it. Researchers in Sweden found that acrylamide, a chemical which is classified as a probable human carcinogen and is known to cause benign and stomach tumors in animal test, was formed when carbohydrate-rich foods such as potatoes, rice or cereals are heated and overheated. The study found that an ordinary bag of crisp may contain up to 500 times more of the substance than the top level allowed in drinking water by the World Health Organization (WHO). While French fries contained up to 100 times the one microgram per liter maximum permitted by the WHO in drinking water.

I remember once when I was trying to find myself and did a second degree in Conservation (which I never completed). I had to do an essay on radiation. This essay led me to a book which spoke about the powerful radioactive effect microwaves have on food. It further went on to explain how microwaves destroy the delicate chemical bonds of food. For a long time after that I did not use a microwave again and discouraged the use of microwaves by my family.

When I read Dr. Emoto, author of *The True Power of Water*, findings about the effects of microwaves on food I was intrigued (please read the first Principle of Wellness to read more about this amazing man, his revolutionary experiments and findings). He took distilled water which he has proven would normally form beautiful crystals and heated it in a microwave for fifteen seconds. The water formed no crystals only "grotesque shapes.

From his experiments Mr. Emoto concluded "the electromagnetic waves of microwave ovens are quite strong. By exposing water to the waves for just fifteen seconds, the good Hado (energy) of the distilled water was destroyed completely. He then took a homemade burger and compared three different cooking methods by using a Hado (energy measuring) machine. The methods used were: frying or microwaving for a normal amount of time (two minutes); microwaving for an excessive amount of time (three minutes). Needless to say the burger that had been pan fried fared the best, while the burger that had been exposed to excessive microwave waves fared the worst.

Enjoy local food

When I lived in the UK there was a growing push to eat food that was grown by local growers. Recently when I lived in Trinidad I always tried to buy food that was locally grown. My mother and I did a little experiment where we compared the taste of locally grown veg and fruit to those that had been brought into the country from the US and other places. The results were interesting and I suppose to be expected. We found that the locally grown fruit and veg tasted better, and sweeter. Much research has shown that food that is not locally produced and has to be brought into a country goes through a process that causes the food to lose much of its nutritional value. In other words it becomes energetically depleted.

Chew well

Chewing food slowly is to eat with total appreciation. When we eat with appreciation we aid in the production of good nutritional food essence. Eating food slowly begins the digestive process. It stimulates the digestive system into action and the digestive enzyme, amylase, moistens the chewed food breaking it down even further.

Eat in a social environment

Have you ever tried eating when you are feeling seriously uptight? It's difficult, isn't it? One of the most ancient principles to good digestion is "to eat in a social setting". Social means to eat with company. If you have to eat alone do not sit in front of the TV or while doing other activities like talking on the phone. Social also means to eat in a relaxed atmosphere. This puts a no on eating in the full height of negative emotions, eating when stressed, or when just feeling seriously tense. Just a little note on eating in front of the TV. Overwhelming evidence has shown that this activity is linked to the growing rate of obesity in society.

Cook with love

I remember once dining in a London restaurant with my family where the food always tasted good. It was a small family owned business where the husband managed and the wife cooked. The food was so delicious it was hard pushed to get a table at this restaurant. I have many fond memories of eating there. There was another restaurant just around the corner from our regular one where the food always tasted bad. It was a bigger more faceless establishment where the staff was quite unfriendly. We ate there twice and never again.

What was the difference with these two places – love? Food cooked with love is vibrationally good food. It is food that taste "sweet" to the palate and goes down well in the stomach. So let's try to avoid cooking when we are angry, upset or feeling negative. Let's also try to avoid eating at food places that have not cooked with our best health interest at heart.

Remember the rice experiment mentioned in Principle 1 where hundreds of families in Japan labeled one rice with the negative words "you fool" and the other bottle of rice "thank you". The former only stagnated slightly and the latter rotted and turned black. It shows that love does make a difference.

Creating good food essence by eating the right nutritional foods

What about vitamins, minerals, carbohydrates, proteins, and so on. Well I don't want you to get too bogged down in these, but it is worth knowing a little about what is a healthy carbohydrate, protein etc.

Macro and micro nutrients

All our meals need to be a balance of Macro nutrients: carbohydrates, protein and fats and Micro nutrients: vitamins and minerals. This can be obtained by eating a varied and balanced diet. There has been much confusion touted around regarding carbohydrates, proteins and fats along with other food items such as sugar. So let's look at these things very carefully and become our own experts.

Macro Nutrients

Carbohydrates

Carbohydrates are a must in the diet. The problem is that most of us think of carbohydrate foods as being bad for our health. However, the carbohydrates that fall into this category are refined denatured grains or foods made from them. So refined white rice, pasta, pizza, doubles, roti, bakes (or dumplings), white flour and all its by products such as biscuits, white bread, cakes – are definitely bad for us. However, the story of carbohydrates is much wider than this. The first thing to understand is – why carbohydrates? Carbohydrates provide energy for all the body's activities. As they are digested carbohydrates are broken down into simple sugars such as glucose. Glucose supplies energy for most of the body's activities. In some cells/tissues such as red blood cells and the brain it is actually the main source of energy. Carbohydrates are needed for building the non-essential amino acids that the body uses to create proteins. They also help in the processing of fat and in the building of cartilage, bone and tissues of the nerve.

Fiber An Important Part Of The Carbohydrate Story

To talk about the importance of fiber it is important to understand a few basic things about our digestive process. We each possess a gastrointestinal tract which is 30 feet long. It connects the mouth to the anus. This tract is what we depend on for: the extraction of nutrients of food we eat, protection from food-borne toxins and the elimination of waste. The gastrointestinal tract is made up of: the esophagus, stomach, small intestine (consisting of the duodenum, jejunum and the ileum, and the large intestine (extends from the ileum to the anus and also comprises
of the colon).

If any part of the gastrointestinal tract is compromised due to diet and lifestyle the ability to properly breakdown foods into small absorb-able components, and to sort out toxic food substance from non toxic food substance is compromised. The result is intestinal toxicity which relates to the presence or production of various toxins in the gastrointestinal tract and their absorption in the blood supply system. In intestinal toxicity individuals may have the following symptoms: gastrointestinal pain, flatulence (gas), bloating, diarrhea, headaches, skin problems, bad breath, fatigue, nervous system disorders, changes in brain function, kidney problems, liver disturbances, constipation to name but a few symptoms.

Besides doing all the right things in terms of how we take things into our body. It is equally important to pay attention to what we take into our body. Fiber is the key to ensuring that our waste matter does not stay in the gastro intestinal tract longer than it needs to. For many of us our digested food matter is moving too slowly in the gastrointestinal tract and lingering longer than it needs to in the last part of the intestines, and colon. This is called the "transit" time. The elimination of waste products should be between 24 hours to 36 hours. However, for most of us it can be up to 150 hours and for many people up to six days.

When food stays in our gastro intestinal tract for so long bacteria such as Clostridium para putrificum can produce intestinal toxicity and illness. These bacteria have the ability to metabolize unabsorbed nutrients or food by products like bile acids, cholesterol or fatty acids and convert them into toxic substances such as carcinogens (cancer producing agents).

There are two types of fiber: soluble and insoluble. Soluble fiber can dissolve in water. It helps slow down the breakdown of complex carbohydrates, such as starch, into simple sugars such as glucose. This helps to slow down the absorption of sugar into the blood. During digestion soluble fiber forms a gel like mass that binds cholesterol to the stools. Eaten in sufficient quantities it helps to reduce cholesterol. Good sources of soluble fiber include oats, barley, rye, fruits, vegetables and pulses. Insoluble fiber cannot be dissolved in water and is not digested or absorbed by the body. Insoluble fiber helps keep the intestinal tract clean by promoting regular bowel movements. It also draws water from the stools and makes them bulkier and softer. A good source of insoluble fiber is: seeds, pulses, skins of vegetables and fruit, whole meal bread or whole grain cereals.

In summary a fiber rich diet is said to:
- Shorten the intestinal transit time
- Create a more bulky stool which moves quicker through the system
- Lower the absorption of potential carcinogens
- Reduce the conversion of bile salts to potentially carcinogenic sterols
- Reduces cholesterol. As fiber has a binding function which binds substances like cholesterol to it.
- Improves healthy gut flora

The best form of carbohydrates to eat are complex carbohydrates such as vegetables, grains, root vegetables which release sugar slowly into the blood (especially good for those with diabetes). Complex carbohydrates contain numerous health benefits including being full of vitamins, minerals, phyto chemicals, protein, and fiber. They are also an excellent source of energy for the body. Also fruit are a good part of the carbohydrate family. They are classed as simple carbohydrates and as we know fruit are also wonderful for keeping us in good form. As we have already said, refined carbohydrates are grains and foods which have been stripped of all their nutritional goodness. Therefore, they compromise the digestive and physical integrity of the body.

When choosing carbohydrates chose:
- Whole meal bread and pasta.
- Whole unrefined grains and cereals
- Limit consumption of refined carbohydrates such as: cakes, biscuits, sweets and sweetened drinks
- Eat plenty of fruit and vegetables (with skin on where possible)

Healthy carbohydrate choices over unhealthy carbohydrate choices

Unhealthy CARB choices	healthy CARB choices
White bread	Whole meal bread
White rice	Brown rice
Croissant	Whole meal muffin
Pearl barley	Pot barley
Apple juice drink (from box)	Freshly juiced apple, or stewed apple or apple on own
Chips	Jacket potato
Sweet corn	Lentils
Fried tortilla chips	Baked tortilla chips
Crackers	Oatcakes, sesame cakes
Cornflake cereal	Muesli (pre-soaked)
Instant porridge	Traditional porridge
White pasta	Whole grain pasta
Egg noodles	Soba noodles
Couscous	Bulgar wheat
Wheat products (when allergic to gluten)	Gluten free products (if suffering from gluten allergy. Weight gain when eating flour products seems to be a sign of mild gluten intolerance)

Protein

Protein is crucial to our diets. It helps to give structure to our cells and is important in cell growth. Like carbohydrates and fats (which we will talk about next) protein is a source of energy in the body. The protein that we eat is broken down into amino acids and peptides (chains of amino acids) and then absorbed into the bloodstream. This pool of amino acids provides most of the elements that are needed to build new proteins in the body.

In the West many of us verge on paranoia about obtaining our quota of protein. But the truth is that in the West protein deficiency is not really an issue. In fact, many of us may have a protein overload as we often have a high intake of meat. One of the important things to realize – protein cannot be stored by the body. Excess protein has to be broken down and disposed off. The liver removes the nitrogen from amino acids so that they can be burned as fuel, and the nitrogen is incorporated into urea, the substance that is excreted by the kidneys. Excess protein intake can overwork and over tax our organs. Foods that we tend to consume for our protein (such as meat) are often high in saturated fat, lack carbohydrate and dietary fiber. The result longer intestinal transit times and a rise in intestinal toxicity.

It is better to reduce your meat intake and receive a good portion of your dietary protein from plants in the form of pulses, nuts, seeds and grains. There is no question that a good well planned vegetarian diet is healthier and provides us with all the nutrients we require without the saturated fats, cholesterol, and contaminants found in animal flesh, eggs and dairy products. The American Dietetic Association states vegetarians have "lower rates of death from ischemic heart disease, lower cholesterol levels, lower blood pressure, and lower rates of hypertension, type 2 diabetes, and prostrate and colon cancer" and vegetarians are less likely than meat eaters to be "obese".

Also studies have shown that children with a well planned vegetarian diet grow taller and higher IQs than their class mates. They have a reduced risk of heart disease, obesity, diabetes and other diseases in the long term. Studies have also shown that even older people who switch to a vegetarian diet can reverse many chronic ailments.

The general consensus is that we need only 0.75g of protein per 1kg (2 ½ 1bs) of body weight. Therefore a man who weights 82 kg (1801bs) needs to consume about 61g of protein per day and a woman weighing 68kg (1501bs) needs an intake of 51g of protein each day.

Fat

We hear so much bad press about fat that I believe most of us are confused about the role fat plays in our diet. Fats form a major part in the integrity of our cell membranes and play a vital role in the absorption of fat soluble vitamins A, D, E and K. Fat gives the body insulation, helping it to maintain a constant temperature against extremes of hot and cold. It also serves as an important source of energy.

Fats are referred to as "good or bad" fats depending on whether their chemical bonds are "saturated" with hydrogen. Unsaturated fats are further classified into mono- and polyunsaturates, which differ in their nutritional makeup.

Saturated Fat

Red meat, other meat products such as sausages, milk, dairy, ice cream and cheese are major sources of saturated fat. Excessive intake of saturated fat has been linked with increase risk of cardiovascular disease by raising the unhealthy LDL levels. So these food items need to be reduced in our diets.

Unsaturated Fat, Mono saturated: Unsaturated fats are divided into mono and polyunsaturates. A diet high in monounsaturated fats helps lower LDL (Low Density Lipo protein) which is the compound cholesterol attaches itself to in order to circulate in the blood. While decreasing LDL, mono-saturated fats do not decrease the good high density protein (HDL). This is good since low HDL and high LDL increase the risk of cardiovascular disease. Dietary sources of mono saturated fats include: nuts, avocados and plant oils. Oils high in mono saturated fat are very good for cooking because they develop fewer free radicals than poly saturated oils when they are heated. Olive oil, Rapeseed oil, sesame and groundnut oil are the highest in mono saturated fats, with olive oil being the highest.

Polyunsaturated fat has two major health components: Omega 3 and Omega 6. These are known as essential fatty acids because they cannot be made by the body. Omega 3 fatty acids are found in oils from cold-water fish such as herring, sardines, and tuna. These essential fatty acids are crucial for regulating blood pressure, blood clotting, immune response, and normal functioning of the brain, spinal cord, and retina of the eye. Omega 6 fatty acids are found in most vegetable oils. These essential fatty acids are crucial for growth, cell structure and the maintenance of a healthy immune system.

Trans-fatty acids: We may have heard this term banded around quite a lot. Trans fatty acids occur when liquid vegetable oils are converted into semi solid fats during the manufacturing process of some types of margarine. Trans fatty acids are most commonly found cakes, pastries, biscuits, meat pies, sausages, crackers and take-away foods. They behave like saturated fat in the body raising cholesterol and generally not contributing to the health of the body.

See the Healthy Protein and Fat Charts on the next page.

Choosing healthy fats

Fat Type	Effect on Body	Sources
Saturated	Raises LDL (Low Density Lipo Protein)	Red meat, meat, and dairy products
Trans-fatty acids	Raises cholesterol and behaves like saturated fat.	Margarine, pastrieds, biscuits, meat pies, sausages, crackers and take-away foods.
Unsaturated Fat		
Monounsaturated Fat	Lowers LDL (Low Density Lipo Protein) and thus cholesterol	Vegetable oils, nuts, avocados
Polyunsaturated Fat: Omega 3	Regulates blood pressure, blood clotting, immune response and normal functioning of the brain, spinal cord and retina	Cold water fish such as herring, sardines and tuna.
Polyunsaturated Fat: Omega 6	Essential for growth of cell, helps maintain the integrity of the cell structure and keeps the immune system healthy.	Plant oils

Healthy fat choices over unhealthy fat choices

Healthy fat choices	Unhealthy fat choices
Plant oils, olive oil, sesame oil, coconut oil, sunflower oil, rapeseed oil, almond oil, corn oil	Red meat and meat. If you are going to eat meat choose organic meat, chicken breast without the skin or chicken without the skin, turkey breast without the skin, goats meat
Fish (remember farmed wild salmon is high in mercury)	Dairy: cow's milk, cheese, margarine, ice cream
Nuts such as: almonds, pistachios	

Micro nutrients

Besides our macro nutrients (which in reality contain many micro nutrients) we need our micro nutrients (minerals and vitamins).

Let's look at vitamins first.

Vitamins

Vitamins are complex organic substances that are needed in very small amounts for many of the essential processes carried out in the body. Usually only a few milligrams (mg) or micrograms (µg) are needed per day, but these amounts are essential for health. Most vitamins cannot be made by the body, so have to be provided by the diet. An exception is vitamin D which can be obtained by the action of sunlight on the skin. Small amounts of a B vitamin (niacin) can be made from the amino acid, tryptophan.

Vitamins have a variety of functions in the body: some are co-factors in enzyme activity, some are antioxidants (prevent oxygen from doing damage in the body) and one (vitamin D) is a pro-hormone. If insufficient amounts of vitamins are available to the body because of a poor diet or some medical condition (e.g. mal absorption of nutrients), specific symptoms will appear and can develop into a deficiency disease. Vitamin deficiency diseases are rare in the UK, but still occur in some parts of the world.

Vitamins have been traditionally grouped into two categories: the fat soluble vitamin, and the water soluble vitamins. Originally, vitamins were given letters (A, B, C, etc.) but now are usually referred to by their chemical names, e.g. folate.

Fat Soluble Vitamins

Vitamin A

Vitamin A is essential to the normal structure and function of the skin and mucous membranes (e.g. lining the digestive system and lungs). It is also required for cell differentiation and therefore for normal growth and development, and for normal vision and for the immune system. Deficiency leads to poor vision in dim light and eventually to blindness. Vitamin A is found in two forms: as retinol in foods from animal sources, and as carotenoids in foods from plant sources, beta carotene being the most common carotenoid. Beta carotene can be converted to retinol in the body; 6mg of beta carotene is equivalent to 1mg of retinol. The total vitamin A content of the diet (from both animal and plant sources) is normally expressed as retinol equivalents.

Excess retinol intake can be toxic. There is evidence that high levels of retinol may increase the risk of birth defects. It is for this reason that women who are pregnant, or who might become pregnant, are advised not to take high-dose vitamin A supplements unless they are advised to do so by a health professional. Liver and liver products may contain a large amount of vitamin A, so these should also be avoided.

Retinol is found in liver, whole milk, cheese and butter. Carotenes are found in milk, carrots, dark green leafy vegetables and orange coloured fruits, e.g. mango and apricots. In the UK, the law states that margarine must be fortified with vitamin A (and vitamin D). Vitamin A is also often voluntarily added to low and reduced fat spreads, as is vitamin D.

With the switch to lower fat dairy products and the lack of popularity of liver these days, there is evidence that retinol intakes have fallen. Carotenoid intake is largely dependent on fruit and vegetable intake and some people's intake of these foods is low. Currently there is concern about the vitamin A intake of some groups. For example, among British women, 15% of those aged 19 – 24 years and 10% of those aged 25 – 34 years were found to have a vitamin A intake below the LRNI; national survey data found that up to 20% of older girls and 13% of older boys in Britain also had intakes below the LRNI.

Vitamin D

Vitamin D is found in foods in two main forms, mostly as cholecalciferol and in small amounts as ergocalciferol. Vitamin D is also made by the action of ultra violet rays on the skin and this is the most important source for the majority of people as few foods contain significant amounts of vitamin D. Vitamin D is converted into another (active) form in the liver and then undergoes further changes in the kidney. In this form it works as a hormone in controlling the amount of calcium absorbed by the intestine. It is also essential for the absorption of phosphorus and for normal bone mineralization and structure. Vitamin D is also involved in the process of cell division. Deficiency of vitamin D leads to skeletal deformity in children (rickets) and to pain and bone weakness in adults (osteomalacia). In the UK, some groups of people (e.g. older Asian adults, Asian women and Asian children) are at risk of vitamin D deficiency because of low vitamin D intake from food and/or inadequate exposure of skin to sunshine. Vitamin D occurs naturally in some animal products including oily fish, eggs, butter and meat. Margarine is fortified with vitamin D (by law) and it is added voluntarily to other fat spreads and some breakfast cereals.

The vitamin D status of subgroups of the populations has been shown to be poor. Particularly at risk are housebound or institutionalized older people who aren't able to benefit from exposure to sunshine. However, poor status has also been found in children, emphasizing the importance of balancing the need for vitamin D synthesis with the use of sun screen, which potentially blocks this process.

Vitamin E

Vitamin E is a group of compounds called tocopherols, of which alpha tocopherol is the most active. It acts as an antioxidant and is required to protect cells against oxidation damage by free radicals, for example oxidation of the lipids in the cell membranes. Epidemiological studies suggest that vitamin E may reduce the risk of some types of cancers and heart disease but this is the subject of on-going debate. The amount of vitamin E needed in the diet is related to the amount of polyunsaturated fatty acids consumed. Since vegetable oils are rich sources of both, deficiency is rare.

Vitamin K

Vitamin K is found in foods from both plant and animal sources and is also made by bacteria in the gut. Vitamin K is essential for the clotting of blood and is required for normal bone structure. Deficiency is very rare in adults, but is sometimes seen in new-born babies. To prevent this, vitamin K is normally given routinely after birth.

Water Soluble Vitamins

Ascorbic Acid (Vitamin C)

Ascorbic acid is a water soluble vitamin required for normal structure and function of connective tissue (in skin, cartilage and bone) as it is involved in the production of collagen - the protein in connective tissue. It is therefore involved in the healing process. It is also involved in the normal structure and function of blood vessels and neurological function. Vitamin C also contributes to the absorption of iron, particularly from non-haem sources such as plant foods. This vitamin also has anti-oxidant activities, potentially protecting cells from free radical oxidation damage. Severe deficiency leads to scurvy. This disease is characterized by bleeding gums, poor wound healing and damage to bone and other tissues. It is rarely seen in Britain today, although it may occur very occasionally in older adults.

If the body is under stress, ascorbic acid is used up more quickly. Smoking is one such stress, and smokers should ensure they eat foods and drinks containing vitamin C.

Ascorbic acid is found almost exclusively in foods from plant sources, although fresh milk and liver contain small amounts.

Thiamin Vitamin B

Thiamin is needed to release energy from carbohydrate. The amount required is related to the amount of carbohydrate eaten. It is involved in the normal function of the nervous system and the heart. Deficiency of thiamin causes beri-beri, a disorder of the nervous system, which occurs in communities where white rice is the main food eaten. A different type of thiamin deficiency affecting brain function is sometimes seen in alcoholics, where daily thiamin intake is low and absorption and utilization of the vitamin is impaired. Thiamin is found in whole grains, nuts and meat.

Riboflavin (vitamin B2)

Riboflavin is required to release energy from protein, carbohydrate and fat. It is also involved in the transport and metabolism of iron in the body and is needed for the normal structure and function of mucous membranes and skin. Although there is no specific deficiency disease, low intakes lead to dryness and cracking of the skin around the mouth and nose. Excess riboflavin is excreted in the urine. Major dietary sources of riboflavin are milks, eggs, fortified breakfast cereals, liver and green vegetables. National survey data indicate that a significant number of teenagers and young women have low intakes of riboflavin.

Niacin

Niacin (nicotinic acid) is found in most foods. It can also be made by the body from the amino acid tryptophan. It is required for the release of energy from food, for the normal structure of the skin and mucous membranes and for normal functioning of the nervous system

Deficiency results in a disease called pellagra. It may occur in communities where maize forms the staple diet. Maize contains very little tryptophan and the niacin that is present is in an unavailable form. If, however, the maize is cooked in a particular way, the niacin is released.

Nicotinic acid is sometimes prescribed by doctors (as a drug) to treat high blood lipid levels, i.e., hyperlipidaemia (excess fat in the blood). But excess intakes can be toxic.

Vitamin B6

Vitamin B6 (comprises of 3 forms – pyridoxine, pyridoxal and pyridoxamine) is essential as a co factor in the metabolism of protein. It is also involved in iron metabolism and transport. Together with folate and vitamin B12, vitamin B6 is required for maintenance of normal blood homocysteine levels. Raised homocysteine is a risk factor for cardiovascular disease. Deficiency may occur as a complication of disease and drug effects. Long term high intakes from supplements have been reported to lead to sensory nerve damage.

Vitamin B6 is found in a variety of foods: beef, fish and poultry are rich sources. It also occurs in eggs, whole-grains and some vegetables.

Vitamin B12

Vitamin B12 (cyanocobalamin) is required for normal cell division and normal blood formation and function. It is also needed for the normal structure and function of nerves. Together with folate and vitamin B6, it is required for the maintenance of normal blood homocysteine levels; raised blood homocysteine is a risk factor for cardiovascular disease. Dietary deficiency is rare, although it is sometimes seen in vegans who obtain virtually no vitamin B12 in their diet unless it is supplemented. Deficiency is also caused by a lack of intrinsic factor - the substance needed for the absorption of vitamin B12. This leads to a type of pernicious anemia in which red cells are enlarged (megaloblastic), and to neurological damage.

Dietary intake is exclusively from animal sources, e.g. milk, meat and eggs (and fortified foods). Although some algae and bacteria can make vitamin B12, it is probably not in a form that can be used by the body. Fortified breakfast cereals can be a useful source of this vitamin.

Folate

The term folate describes a group of derivatives of pteroyl glutamic acid. Folic acid is the synthetic form of the vitamin and the most stable. It is used in supplements and for food fortification. Various folates are found in both plant and animal foods. Folate is essential for normal cell division and in the formation of blood cells. It is also needed for the normal structure of the nervous system and specifically in the development of the neural tube (which develops into the spine and skull) in the developing embryo.

Together with vitamins B6 and B12, folate is involved with the maintenance of normal blood homocysteine levels. The amino acid homocysteine is an intermediate in folate metabolism and there is a strong body of evidence suggesting that raised blood homocysteine is an independent risk factor for heart disease and stroke. It is not yet clear, however, whether folate supplementation can reduce heart disease risk. Folates are found in liver, yeast extract, orange juice and green leafy vegetables. Various foods, e.g. breakfast cereals and bread may be fortified with folic acid (the synthetic form of folate).

Deficiency of folate leads to megaloblastic anaemia and may be due to poor diet or increased requirement, e.g. in pregnancy, from drug interaction or as a result of malabsorption. There is conclusive evidence that increasing intakes of folate through supplements of folic acid, before conception and during the first twelve weeks of pregnancy, prevents the majority of neural tube defects (e.g. spina bifida) in babies. It is recommended that all women of childbearing age, and especially those planning a pregnancy and who are in the early stages of pregnancy, take a daily supplement of 400μg folic acid as it is difficult to achieve this amount of additional folate by diet alone. Women's diets typically provide about 250 ìg folate/day.

In some parts of the world, e.g. USA and Canada, folic acid is added by law to flour and bread. The UK and the rest of Europe has yet to agree this step, largely because of concerns that fortification might mask the symptoms of B12 deficiency in older people, among whom B12 deficiency is quite common. The government's advisory committee, SACN, is currently re-looking at the folate issue and is likely to report in 2005.

Minerals

Minerals are needed for a variety of body functions. The British National Diet and Nutrition Survey (NDNS) have revealed that a minority in the population has low levels of minerals e.g. potassium, magnesium and zinc. This is particularly true of the sick, teenagers, young adults and older adults. Does that sound like it covers most of us to you? The crucial minerals we all need in our diets are:

Calcium

Calcium is the main constituent of hydroxyapatitie, the principle mineral in the bone and teeth. Calcium also plays an essential role in intracellular signaling and is therefore necessary for nerve and muscle function. It is also involved in blood clotting.

The absorption and excretion of calcium are controlled by several hormones and by vitamin D. Insufficient calcium in bones can result from an inadequate supply of vitamin D which is essential for absorption. In children, vitamin D deficiency results in rickets and in adult osteomalacia, in which bones become weak owing to lack of calcium. There is evidence that there is a significant portion of young women who have an average intake below normal. An adequate intake of calcium is vital for health, particularly in times of growth e.g. childhood, adolescence, pregnancy and also during lactation.

Foods that are particularly rich in calcium are milk, cheese and other dairy products (but not butter), vegetables such as broccoli, and spinach.

Peak bone mass (PBM) is reached by the age of about 30 years, with 90-95% reached by 20 years. After this age, some loss of calcium from bone is normal and bone mass slowly decreases. However, severe loss causes the bones to become weak, brittle and to break easily. This condition is known as osteoporosis.

Osteoporosis occurs if large amounts of bone (not just calcium) are lost, or if the bones are not strong before bone loss begins. It most frequently affects older women who have gone through the menopause (oestrogen has a protective effect on bone), although men can also be affected. Currently, it is believed that 1 in 3 women and 1 in 8 men aged over 50 will suffer some degree of osteoporosis during their

Certain groups of people may have higher requirements for specific vitamins, e.g. those suffering from medical conditions, recovering from illness, smokers, athletes and pregnant women. These people need to ensure they obtain adequate intakes by eating foods rich in particular vitamins. Occasionally vitamin supplementation will be useful, e.g. folic acid is advised for women planning a baby.

Magnesium

Magnesium is present in all tissues including bone. It is required for normal energy metabolism and electrolyte balance. It is also needed for muscle function and for bone and tooth structure. It is present in all foods but as magnesium is found in chlorophyll, the green pigment in plants, it is abundant in dark green leafy vegetables, but much of it is bound and not readily available for absorption. Grains and nuts are also rich in magnesium. Although deficiency is rare, low intakes have been observed in some groups, e.g. one in five women aged 19-34 years. Teenagers are also at risk of low intakes with just over half of teenage girls having intakes below the LRNI (51% of 11-14 age group and 53% of 15-18 age groups) and more than 20% of boys aged 11-14 years are at risk of low intakes.

Phosphorus

Phosphorus is present in all plant and animal cells, and 80% of the phosphorus in the body is present as calcium salts in the skeleton. It is essential for bone and tooth structure, for the structure of cell membranes (in phospholipids) and for energy metabolism.

Sodium

Sodium helps regulate body water content and electrolyte balance, and is involved in energy utilization and nerve function. It is also required for the absorption of certain nutrients and water from the gut. Too much salt in the diet is associated with an increased risk of raised blood pressure, which is a risk factor for heart disease and stroke. A low salt diet may be used in the treatment of hypertension.

Excess sweating, e.g. due to exercise in a hot environment, may cause some sodium depletion; sodium intakes may need to increase modestly and temporarily to replenish the loss in sweat.

Most raw foods contain very small amounts of sodium chloride (salt). But salt is often added during the processing, preparation, preservation and serving of foods. The average intake of salt amongst many adults is 11.0 g/day for adult men and 8.1 g/day for adult women, compared with the recommendation of 6 g per day in adults. Intakes among children are also higher than recommended. Work is under way to reduce the amount of salt present in the food supply. For example, a reduction in bread, soups and snacks has already been achieved and industry targets have been set for other foods, including meat products and biscuits.

The public also has a role to play in restricting the addition of salt to their food in the kitchen and at the table. About 20% of salt consumed is added at home during cooking and at the table.

Potassium

Potassium is found in body fluids and is essential for water and electrolyte balance and for the proper functioning of cells, including nerves. It is present in almost all foods (vegetables and milk are rich sources). Processed foods typically contain less than raw foods. Potassium has a beneficial blood pressure-lowering effect in people with raised blood pressure.

Low dietary potassium intakes have been observed amongst adults like those in the UK the where about 1 in 5 women had intakes below the Recommended Nutritional Intake (RNI) and in common with some other minerals, potassium intakes were lower among younger women. About 1 in 5 11-14 year old girls and about 2 in 5 15–18 year old girls were found in the UK to have low intakes of potassium.

Iron

Iron is required for the formation of hemoglobin in red blood cells, which transport oxygen around the body. Iron is also required for normal energy metabolism, and for metabolism of drugs and foreign substances that need to be removed from the body. The immune system also requires iron for normal function

A lack of iron leads to low iron stores in the body and eventually to iron deficiency anemia. Loss of blood due to injury or large menstrual losses increases iron requirements. Women of child bearing age and teenage girls, in particular, need to ensure their diet supplies enough iron as their requirements are higher than those of men of the same age. Women in all age groups, except for older women (over the age of 54 years) often have lower levels of iron than what is recommended. A very significant proportion of younger women (2 out of 5) have intakes below the lower reference nutrient intake (LRNI) i.e. intakes that are likely to be inadequate.

Iron is found in animal and plant sources. Iron from animal sources (haem iron) is better absorbed than iron from plant sources (non-haem iron). Absorption of non-haem iron is affected by various factors in food. Phytate (in cereals and pulses), fibre, tannins (in tea) and calcium can all bind non-haem iron in the intestine, which reduces absorption. On the other hand vitamin C, present in fruit and vegetables, aids the absorption of this kind of iron when eaten at the same time. The same applies to meat, fish and poultry.

Trace Elements

Zinc

Zinc is present in many enzymes and is essential for cell division and, therefore, for growth and tissue repair. It is also necessary for normal reproductive development. Zinc is also required for the functioning of the immune system and in the structure and function of the skin and, therefore, in wound healing. In some countries, delayed puberty and small stature have been linked to zinc deficiency, though it is not certain that this is due to zinc alone.

Iodine

Iodine is used to make thyroid hormones. The thyroid hormones control many metabolic processes and if there is insufficient iodine in the diet, the result is lethargy and swelling of the thyroid gland in the neck to form a goiter. Iodine is also required for normal neurological development and for energy metabolism. Infants born of severely iodine deficient mothers may be mentally retarded (cretinism). Nowadays iodine deficiency is universally rare.

The amount of iodine in plant foods such as vegetables and cereal grains is determined by the iodine level of the environment, i.e. the amount in the soil or water. The only rich sources of iodine are sea-foods, but in some countries certain foods, e.g. salt and bread, are fortified with iodine.

Fluoride

Fluoride is found in few foods but in varying quantities in water. The addition of fluoride to toothpaste is now very common and is important in those areas where the water supply is low in fluoride. It contributes to the maintenance of bone health by supporting bone mineralization and it protects teeth against dental decay (caries). Very large amounts of fluoride can cause mottling and crumbling of teeth, and changes to the bones - a condition called fluorosis. In some water supplies around the world where the fluoride content is low fluoride is added in small amounts (about 1 part per million [ppm]).

Selenium

Selenium is a component of some of the enzymes which protect the body against damage due to oxidation (free radical mediated damage). It is also necessary for the use of iodine in thyroid hormone production and for immune system function. Selenium deficiency has been linked with a form of heart disease (Keshan disease) in parts of China where soil levels of selenium are very low. It has been suggested that low levels of intake may be associated with the increased risk of some cancers but the 1998 *COMA working group on diet and cancer did not find sufficient evidence for this link. Sources of selenium include cereals, fish, eggs and Brazil nuts.

Copper

Copper is a constituent of many enzyme systems and the body needs copper to be able to use iron properly. It is needed for the structure of connective tissue in bone, the lungs and blood vessels. Good sources of copper include green vegetables, fish, liver and nuts.

Chromium

Chromium is found in a variety of foods and it has been suggested that it may be involved in the action of insulin, the hormone which controls glucose levels in the blood. However, there is still no general agreement for the role of chromium in insulin metabolism.

Manganese

Manganese is required for bone formation and for energy metabolism. It is also a constituent of an antioxidant enzyme, which helps prevent free radical-mediated cellular damage. It is present in plant foods such as vegetables, cereals and nuts. Tea is also a rich source.

Other Minerals

There are other minerals which are needed in tiny amounts and which appear to be essential in the diet, e.g. molybdenum, boron. Others occur in the diet, but whether they are essential is unclear, e.g. nickel, lithium, antimony, aluminum and lead.

Other Nutrient Elements: Phytochemicals

Phytochemicals are also known as phytonutrients. They are the naturally occurring protective chemicals that are found in foods of plant origin. Many studies have shown that there may be as many as 100 phytochemicals in 1 serving of vegetables.

Evidence shows that those who consume a diet rich in fruits, vegetables and plant life (eg herbs), and therefore in phytochemicals, have a lower incidence of many diseases including cancer, diabetes, cardiovascular disease.

Phytochemicals are powerful anti-oxidants therefore protecting the cells from cancer, cardiovascular disease, urinary tract infections, rheumatoid arthritis and reduced immunity.

When and how to supplement?

Most of us are either stressed, ill, recovering from illness, getting older, young, old, living very active lives, eating poor diets, therefore, somewhere and somehow most of have certain vitamins minerals, and phytochemicals missing from our diets. Which ones depend on each individual and their personal physical and life requirements? The good news that beginning to eat a balanced and varied diet goes a long way to getting us back onto the road to good health. However, checking to see what extra supplementation you may need is also a good idea. If you are a vegetarian you will need a supplementation of vitamin B12. The best way to know what micro nutrients are missing from your diet is to check the Nutrient Deficiency charts below.

Nutrient Deficiency Chart

Deficiency	Nutrient	RDI Recommend Daily Intake	
	Minerals	Men	Women
Bone pain, pins and needles in hands and feet, muscle cramps and twitching, convulsions and osteoporosis. Calcium deficiency during childhood leads to irritability, muscle weakness, stunted growth, and muscle cramps and twitching.	Calcium	700 mg	700 mg
Low levels cause: low calcium level and potassium in blood, changes in the digestive system, nervous and muscular systems, heart and circulatory systems and the development of the blood. There are also the following signs: fatigue, weakness, poor appetite, impaired speech, irregular heart rhythms, anemia, and tremors. Affected babies and children may fail to thrive. Rapid Heart rate and compulsion (are the advanced symptoms).	Magnesium	300 mg	270 mg
Muscle weakness and bone pain, anemia, impaired red blood cells, problems with the nervous system including psychological disorders,	Phosphorus	550 mg	550 mg

abnormal excretion of calcium in urine and kidney stones.			
Fatigue, muscle weakness, constipation, cramps, and reduced kidney functions, heart problems (with severely low levels).	Potassium	3500 mg	3500 mg
Headache, nausea and vomiting, muscle cramps, drowsiness, fainting and coma.	Sodium	1600 mg	1600 mg
No deficiency has been detected in humans because the mineral occurs naturally in all foods.	Sulfur	None set	None set
Rare to see deficiency. Those who excessively exercise or are fed through long-term intravenous methods are often deficient.	Chromium	None set	None set
Increased incidence of tooth decay.	Fluoride	None set	None set
Enlarged thyroid gland which leads to under active thyroid (hypothyroidism), goiter (swelling of the neck), slow metabolism, weight gain, learning difficulties amongst children.	Iodine	140 mg	140 mg
Anemia (characterized by weakness and pale skin), fatigue and faintness, cold or numbness in the fingers and toes due to poor blood circulation,	Iron	8.7 mg	14. 8 mg

shortness of breath, greater susceptibility of infections, poor work performance, soft or brittle nails, behavior changes. Young children become tired and have low concentration. They may also develop learning difficulties and behavioral problems.			
Enlarged heart that is not pumping blood sufficiently. It is also thought to have anti-cancerous properties as it blocks enzymes involved in cell division and growth.	Selenium	75 mg	60 mg
Poor appetite, loss of sense of taste, digestive problems, diarrhea, vomiting, night blindness, hair loss, skin problems, poor wound healing, problems with growth in children, delayed onset of puberty and sexual maturation.	Zinc	9.5 mg	7 mg

Deficiency, Vitamin Nutrient and Natural Source Chart

Nutrient deficiency	At Risk Groups	Nutrient Source
Vitamin		
Vitamin A	Pregnant women and infants in developing countries, those who abuse alcohol, sufferers of long term conditions that affect absorption of fat such as cystic fibrosis or Chron's disease. This is because vitamin A is absorbed in fat.	Carrots, cabbage, kale, pumpkin, spinach, peppers, butternut squash, apricots, orange-fleshed melon, mango, liver, eggs.
Vitamin B1	Those who abuse alcohol (alcohol reduces ability for this vitamin to be absorbed).	Peas, spinach, liver, beef, pork, wholemeal bread, nuts, bran flakes, soya beans.
Vitamin B2	Those affected by conditions that affect absorption in the intestine.	Asparagus, okra, milk, yoghurt, meat, eggs, fish.
Niacin	Rare in Western countries as it is a vitamin found in protein rich foods. However those affected include where maize is the essential part of the diet, those who abuse alcohol.	Peas, liver, red meat, poultry, makeral, mullet, salmon, swordfish, kidney beans, peanuts, soya beans.
Vitamin B6	Babies fed on formula that does not contain B6, those who abuse alcohol, cigarette smokers, women who use contraception, some medications for lung infection tuberculosis.	Potatoes, sweet potatoes, bananas, chicken, turkey, mackerel, mullet, salmon, swordfish, trout, tuna.

Vitamin B12	As naturally found only in meat vegetarians and especially vegans are special risk and need to supplement.	Dairy, eggs, beef, seafood.
Biotin	Pregnant women, people who abuse alcohol, those who do not produce sufficient amounts of stomach acid such as old people.	Cauliflower, mushrooms, liver, egg yolks, mackerel, sardines, kidney beans, peanuts, yeast.
Folate	Those who consume a diet that is fatty filled with processed foods and eat very little fruit and vegetables. Also those with intestinal problems, such as Chron's disease, disorders that affect absorption of this vitamin.	Sweet corn, asparagus, Brussels sprouts, cabbage, cauliflower, fresh green vegetables, peas, spinach, oranges, liver, black eye beans, black beans, chick peas, lentils pinto beans, kidney beans.
Vitamin C	Those who do not consume enough fresh citrus fruits and natural juices.	Plantain, Asparagus, Broccoli, Brussels sprouts, Cabbage, Peppers, Tomatoes, Blackberries, Grapefruit, Guava, Kiwi fruit, Mango, Melon, Oranges, Pineapples, Strawberries.
Vitamin D	Older people, those living in cold climates and due to religion or culture cover up, those living in urban areas of high pollution.	Egg yolk, Cod and halibut liver oils, mackerel, salmon, sardines, tuna, natural sunlight.
Vitamin E	People with long term conditions that prevent the absorption of fat from the intestines such as cystic fibrosis or Chron's disease.	Wheatgerm, prawns, almonds, hazelnuts, peanuts, pistachio nuts, soya beans, sunflower seeds.

Vitamin K	People with condition that affects absorption of fats from the intestines, those on long term antibiotics (antibiotics affect gut flora).	Asparagus, broccoli, Brussels sprouts, cabbage, carrots, cauliflower, celery, peas, spinach, apricots, grapes, pears, plums.

Deficiency, Mineral Nutrient and Natural Source Chart

Nutrient deficiency	At Risk Groups	Nutrient Source
Mineral		
Calcium	Children and adolescents. A deficiency can remain undetected for years as bones keep on releasing calcium into the blood to maintain normal levels. This leads to bone disease in the long run.	Cheese, milk, yoghurt, spinach, whitebait and sardines, salmon, almonds, tofu.
Magnesium	Those who suffer from malabsorption, long term use of diuretic medications, excessive vomiting, kidney disease, chronic alcohol abuse, hyper parathyroid ism, and liver cirrhosis.	Whole grains, globe artichokes, spinach, wholemeal bread, bran flakes, lamb's kidneys, red meat, beans and pulses, nuts (such as Brazil nuts, almonds, cashews and peanuts), sunflower seeds, sesame seeds, tofu.
Phosphorus	People who take excessive antacid indigestion medication for prolonged periods.	Whole grains, especially oats, dairy products, red meat, poultry, seafood, pulses (especially lentils), nuts (such as Brazil nuts and almond), sunflower seeds.
Potassium	Those suffering from excessive vomiting, diarrhea or who have kidney disease, metabolic disorders where body chemistry is affected, too many laxatives, or eating disorders such as anorexia nervosa and bulimia nervosa.	Whole grains, potatoes, asparagus, avocados, spinach, tomatoes, bananas, orange-flesh melons, oranges, dairy products, red meat, broad

		beans.
Sodium	Those suffering from prolonged vomiting, diarrhea, periods of prolonged illness.	Sea salt.
Sulfur	No particular group.	Present in all foods.
Chromium	Those suffering from prolonged illness and or long term intravenous feeding. Studies have shown that male runners lose chromium indicating that it is needed with increased exercise.	Potatoes, broccoli, green beans, tomatoes, apples, bananas, grapes, oranges, red meat, turkey.
Copper	Deficiency rare but does occur in those that are malnourished especially young children.	Whole grain foods (especially barley), liver, seafood, (crab, lobsters, oysters), nuts (such as almonds, Brazil nuts, pistachios), sesame.
Fluoride	In areas where fluoride not added to drinking water.	Water.
Iodine	People who do not get enough ionized salts or live in areas where iodine is not found.	
Iron	Pregnant women, breast feeding and new mothers, infants, and children, menstruating females, adolescents, older adults, babies who are not breast feeding, vegetarians whose only source of iron is from plants which is absorbed slower.	Spinach, green leafy vegetables, dried fruit (especially prunes), offal, red meat, egg yolks, poultry, sardines, tuna, prawns, range of pulses (such as red beans, chickpeas, and soya beans).
Selenium	People with malabsorption problems, who rely on intravenous nutrition, malnourished infants and children.	Brown rice, wheatgerm, wholemeal bread, poultry, fish (especially tuna), shell fish (especially oysters),

		Brazil nuts.
Zinc	Those suffering from poor intestinal absorption, people who abuse alcohol, HIV sufferers with infections, diabetics, those on protein restrictive diets, and anyone suffering from liver disease.	Dairy products, red meat, eggs, poultry, crab, lobster, oysters, Brazil nuts, haricot beans, soya beans.

.

Deficiency, Phytochemicals Nutrient and Natural Source Chart

Some key Phytochemicals	Functions	Nutrient Source*
Bioflavonoids	Important for the absorption of vitamin C and to protect it from oxidation (damage).	Citrus fruits such as: orange, lime, grapefruit, lemons. Also many herbs.
Carotenoids	Protect against cardiovascular disease.	Found in orange fruit and vegetables as carrots, melons, sweet potatoes, and butternut squash.
Glucosinolates	Aid in liver detoxification, regulates certain white blood cells important for immunity, and also may help reduce tumor growth especially in the breast, liver, colon, lung, stomach and esophagus.	Found in all vegetables.
Organosulphides	Stimulates anti-cancer enzymes, slow the formation of blood clots, and are excellent immune boosters. This is what gives onions and leak pungent smell.	Found in vegetables.
Phytoestrogens	Protect the body from cardiovascular disease, slows down the progression of cancer, and protects against osteoporosis.	Soya products and linseeds.

Flavonoids	Protect the body from inflammation, allergic reactions, and viral infections.	Present in foods of plant origin.
Indoles	Thought to help prevent breast cancer.	Present in foods of plant origin.
Isoflavones	Help to inhibit estrogen-promoted cancer and lower high levels of blood cholesterol.	Present in foods of plant origin.
Limonoids	Protects against lung disease.	Found in peel of citrus fruit.
lycopene	Protects against cancer of cervix, stomach, bladder , colon, and prostrate diseases.	Found in tomatoes.
Para-coumaric acid	Helps prevent cancer by interfering with the development of cancer causing nitrosamines in stomach.	Found in foods of plant origin.
Phenols polyphenol	Protect plants from chemical damage and does the same for humans.	Found in green tea.
phytosterols	Reduces absorption of cholesterol from the diet and therefore lowers cholesterol levels in blood.	Soya products.
Terpenes	May block action of cancer-causing factors	Found in all foods of

	and may inhibit hormone-related cancers such as ovarian cancer.	to	plant origin.

* Please note phytochemicals are said to be found in all foods of plant origins. The list above is just a guideline.

A Word On Bio availability Of Micro nutrients

It should be clear from everything you have just read about vitamins, minerals and phytochemicals that we need a lot of them. Also most of us because of our fast pace diet and lifestyles seem to be deficient in many micro nutrients. When I went to America, I observed an interesting phenomenon of most people eating vitamins and nutrient pills for breakfast, lunch, dinner and then went on to eat poorly prepared meals or takeouts!

The natural answer to ensuring we have our required dosage of supplementation is to first ensure we are doing all the right things to ensure the food essence created in the stomach and which feeds the rest of the body is "good". So this means doing the things we have read about: eating in the right way so as to keep our digestive fire and digestive track in good working condition. It also means making sure our meals are balanced.

Juice It

Juicing is also a very powerful method of ensuring our cells, tissues, and organs receive instant nourishment. This is something I recommend that we all add into our daily diets. The uplifting and rejuvenating power of juice is truly miraculous. With natural juice, the digestive system gets a chance to rest but receive all the nourishment it needs. This is important as many of us are eating but due to the impairment of the digestive system we are unable to absorb all the nourishment we need from our food. Juicing also provides us with an abundance of fresh enzymes which are necessary for all bio-chemical activity in the body. In one glass of juice you can eat 2 apples, 4 carrots, ¼ beetroot, patchoi and ginger. You can also do this several times a day!

When I started juicing I noticed my skin was glowing, my energy levels were up, creative powers flowing, hunger levels were down (a craving for food is due to nutrients missing from the body particularly micronutrients), I was calmer, my bowel movements were better and I was not waking up as sluggish in the mornings.

Supplement It

When we need to supplement it is important to remember one fact – not all supplements are equal and expensive does not necessarily equal the best. Many supplements are manufactured in tablet form and held together by binders, fillers, protein fragments along with other things which inhibit digestion, thus their metabolism, and their bio-availability to the body. So before you buy any supplement try and look out for the following:

Government guidelines: whichever country your supplements are from ensure that they follow the countries national guidelines. It will say so on the bottle. If it doesn't indicate this then it will in all likely be a poor supplement. Meaning one that passes right through your system.

Natural over Synthetic: Very few people know but many supplements are synthesized predominantly from petrochemicals. However, much clinical evidence has shown that natural forms of vitamins including A, B-complex, C, D and E are more efficiently absorbed by the body and have a more profound effect on deficiencies and disease over their synthetic poorer cousins. So read the label to find out.

It dissolves: Most supplements that meet government standards often have to meet a standard of dissolution. One of the crucial factors for ensuring a supplement dissolves and is bio-available to the body is chelation. Chelation, refers to the process that increases the absorption of minerals such as chromium, copper, iron, magnesium, manganese, molybdenum and zinc. It is a process where the mineral is wrapped in an amino acid making it easier for the body to absorb. A non chelated mineral supplement will have only a 10% absorption rate. When chelated its absorption rate goes up to 45% and more. So when you read the label of your mineral supplement it should have something like Manganese Chelate etc.

And What About SSW?

Sugar, Salt, Water

Sugar

Sugar is an interesting subject. Many of us hear about the adverse effects of sugar but if we are truthful to ourselves we can only name a few vague things about the detrimental effects of sugar. For a long time, I also did not know what they were.

Just so we're in no doubt. Let's start by with the revelation – sugar is classed as one of the most dangerous substances in our modern diet. It is so dangerous it is classed as a "poison". Poison meaning anything that has a negative effect on our body. Sugar is seen as one of the major sources of degenerative illness in the body. It is one of the key causes to the onset of diseases such as diabetes, mental illness and cancer. The dangerous substance of sugar is in the form of sucrose, the white crystalline sugar from cane or beet stripped away of all its minerals, vitamins, protein, fiber and water. The sugar in fruit and milk are nutritional and healthy unlike sucrose (white sugar). The "brown" sugar we buy in shops is far from brown, but is merely white sugar with molasses spun back into it for colour and flavor. Sugars many detrimental effects on the body include:

Immune system suppressant: The intake of sugar causes a rush in the body and a panic. The pancreas secrets large quantities of insulin required to break the sugar down. Insulin does not leave the bloodstream straightaway. It stays in the blood stream long after sugar has been metabolized. Insulin suppresses the release of growth hormone which is the primary regulator of the immune system. Therefore a daily and excessive intake of sugar equals a compromised immune system and illness.

Nutrient robber: Sugar is "nutritionally naked". So the body must borrow missing vitamins, minerals and other synergistic nutrients required to metabolize sugar from its own sugars. Sugar constantly siphons of our nutrients on a deep cellular and tissue level. There is over whelming evidence to show that sugar causes dental decay not because of contact with teeth but by leeching calcium from within. Sugar depletes the body of potassium and magnesium which are required for proper cardiac function and is therefore a major factor in heart disease.

Sugar causes cravings: because sugar depletes the body of its nutrients it produces intense food cravings and sends us on an eating binge as the body seeks to replenish nutrients robbed from it. Sugar's many detrimental effects on the body include:

Sugar causes mental and social problems: Sugar effects orderly brain function. Orderly brain function is controlled by glutamic acid, a vital compound found in many vegetables. B Vitamins play a major role in dividing glutamic acid into antagonistic-complementary compounds which produce a "proceed" or "control" factor response in the brain. B vitamins are also manufactured by symbiotic bacteria which live in our intestines. When these bacteria die because of fermentation caused in the intestinal tract by sugar our Vitamin B stock runs low resulting in memory loss, sleepiness, and mental lethargy. In Mega Vitamin B3 Therapy for Schizophrenia, Dr. Abram Hoffer states, "patients are also advised to follow a good nutritional program with restriction of sucrose and sucrose rich foods". It has been found that many learning difficulties and disruptive behavior by children and adults is due to the high intake of sugar in our "modern" diets.

Sugar causes obesity: Excess sugar is initially stored in our liver in the form of glucose (glycogen). Since the liver's capacity is limited, a daily intake of refined sugar (above the required amount of natural sugar) causes the liver to expand like a balloon. When the liver is filled to its capacity, the excess glucose (glycogen) is returned to the blood in the form of fatty acids. These are taken to every part of the body and stored in the most inactive areas: the belly, the buttocks, the breast and the thighs.

Sugar causes organ damage: When the liver has dumped excess glucose (glycogen) in the form of fatty acids in the inactive parts of the body such as the belly, buttocks, breast and thighs. The fatty acids are then dumped in the active organs such as the heart and kidney. These organs slow down and their tissues degenerate and turn into fat. The whole body is affected by reduced function and blood pressure is pushed up.

How much is too much?

Now for even more intimate truths – most of us eat over double the recommended intake of sugar. The recommended daily intake of sugar by the US Department of Agriculture is 40g (11/2 oz). Most of us eat 100grams of sugar every day or 41 kilos in a year. And it gets even more terrible over 80% of the sugars we eat are refined and "hidden" in the "everyday food" we eat such as cereal, fizzy drinks, burgers, and other processed foods. Refined white flour and related products cause a high rise in blood sugar level and are deplete of nutrients.

Read The Label

It is important that we learn to recognize the hidden added sugars in food. It is important that we start to read our labels. Here are all the clever ways manufacturers add sugar into our foods by adding: brown sugar, corn sweetener, corn syrup, dextrose, fructose, fruit juice concentrate, glucose, high-fructose corn syrup, invert sugar, lactose, maltose, malt syrup, molasses, raw sugar, sucrose, syrup, table sugar.

A Word About Natural Sweeteners

The best natural sweeteners are molasses and honey. In Ayurveda honey is said to be a powerful healer. It lowers conditions such as obesity and diabetes and is said to be best taken in cool water. Honey becomes a poison when it is heated up through cooking. Honey is a sweet flavour but it is also an astringent. Unlike refined white sugar, honey and molasses are nutritious to the system.

Salt

Making The Headlines

Salt is back in the headlines. In March 2006 the Food Standards Agency (FSA) published new (voluntary) salt reduction targets for food manufacturers and retailers to reduce salt levels by 2010. Over-consumption of salt is linked to high blood pressure, heart disease and stroke.

The FSA's aim is to encourage the reduction of salt levels in 85 food categories that contribute most of the amount of salt in diets of UK consumers. These include: bread, breakfast cereals, cheese, ready-meals, cakes, biscuits, pastries, bacon and other foods. However, some campaigners argue that the voluntary targets don't go far enough, possibly endangering the lives of thousands of at-risk people. Food manufacturers, represented by the Food and Drink Federation, on the other hand, believe the new the targets present a challenge to the industry.

In 2004 the FSA highlighted the association between salt consumption and high blood pressure with its 'Sid the Slug' campaign. Around 18 million people in the UK have high blood pressure, or hypertension, a symptom-less yet dangerous condition

People with high blood pressure are three times more likely to develop heart disease or have a stroke than people with normal blood pressure. Around 50,000 people a year die from stroke and nearly 238,000 from heart disease in the UK, so cutting average salt consumption could save many lives.

How Much Is Too Much?

Salt is crucial for our health, but currently we eat, on average, at least two and a half times what we need. Governments are trying to reduce average salt consumption for adults from more than 9g a day to no more than 6g. They think levels should be even lower for babies and children, recommending less than 1g per day from 0-6 month; 1g per day from 7-12 months; 2g per day from 1-3 years; 3g per day from 4-6 years; and 5g per day from 7-10 years. These are maximum levels, and they advise parents to aim for less.

Salt, Salt Where Are You Hidden?

Six grams of salt is a level teaspoonful. It's difficult to measure consumption because 65-85% of our salt is already in the foods we eat, and not what we add in cooking and at the table. Bread, breakfast cereals, biscuits, baked beans and ready-meals can be high in salt, alongside more obviously salty-tasting foods such as crisps, bacon, cheese and olives.

Unveiling The Mystery Of The Label

Food labels can be confusing. To find out how much salt is in an item, you need to check the label for sodium, which is the component of salt (sodium chloride), associated with health risks. As a guide, 0.5g or more of sodium per 100g is a high level, below 0.5g is moderate and 0.1g is low. A salty anchovy can go a long way in a bowl of spaghetti, while you can consume a large amount of unnoticed sodium in a curry ready-meal

Both those who agree and disagree with the connection between high blood pressure and salt say that eating plenty of vegetables, fruits and seeds alongside taking exercise, not becoming overweight and not drinking too much alcohol, are other factors important in preventing high blood pressure. Replacing salty processed foods with fresh foods is likely to be beneficial for reasons other than just salt. It is the overall diet and lifestyle that matter, not just one component.

But I Just Love It!

Research has shown that our palates get accustomed to a certain level of salt, but they re-adjust after a few weeks of a lower-salt diet. Food writer Sybil Kapoor, in her book 'Taste' (Mitchell Beazley), was surprised to discover new nuances of taste in everything she ate after she cut down on salt. "Ironically, the less salt we eat, the more salt we can taste in our food," she says. Saltiness is masked by sweetness and enhanced by bitterness and sourness, so adding a squeeze of lemon can make less salty taste stronger, she says.

Water

Water is not a nutrient and many people often forget to write about it. Yet the truth is we are 70% water and unable to survive without it. Water is essential for our body to work properly. It lubricates our joints and eyes, helps us to swallow, provides a medium for most reactions in our body to occur, and picks up calcium and magnesium. It is better to filter water rather than drink it straight from the taps. Filtered water reduces chlorine, and impurities in water. Where clean safe water supply is not available bottled water is highly recommended. But know that many bottled waters on the market are straight from your tap. The hygiene Institute of Yokohama City in Japan did a survey on bottled mineral water sold in the city. Among the thirty items surveyed, fourteen of them were imported from America, France, and Canada, and sixteen were domestic water samples. The water was examined for formaldehyde and acetaldehyde. Aldehydes were detected in nineteen items-five imported and fourteen domestic. Among the nineteen items, seventeen contained both formaldehyde and acetaldehyde. One of the waters from America measured 260 grams per litre of acetaldehyde.

The health of our environment is being compromised and this includes the health of the water we drink. But as Masaru Emoto, a dynamic researcher from Japan showed, we can change the quality of our water just by changing its Hado (energy). By speaking positively over the water we drink, putting positive messages on it he has shown through the crystals water form that it changes its composition all together.

Also there is the whole question to how much water we must drink a day. I have heard many people say "Oh I must drink a litre of water a day". Ayurveda is clear that we must drink and eat when we are thirsty and hungry. In fact, too much water in the body can cause its own set of complications, and we all know about the "weeing" syndrome. And for all of us that are affected by the said syndrome the advice is to "don't drink gallons of water through the day, sip continuously through the day". This was wise advice given to me by a therapist and it seemed to work very well. Because let's be truthful nothing is more annoying than making several pit stops to the bathroom within the space of several seconds.

Now What Do I Do?

If you are feeling confused about all the dietary principles take a deep breath and release all the tension. Changing our diets and outlook to self nourishment of ourselves can feel difficult and let's not talk about challenging. However, it can also be rewarding and fun especially when you are armed with some key principles.

I suggest you read over everything to do with the advice in this section, at least once, twice and three times. As you read over the facts do not try to memorize everything but try to get a general feeling of what is being said. Tune into yourself and see what really resonates with you. You will find that because you have the innate knowledge of what is good for you and what is not, some things will resonate with you and make you nod your head; others will not.

After you have read the advice in this Principle over a few times, it is time to try to put some of it into practice. So where do you start? Don't hesitate; we have not journeyed so far for me to gallop of into the wind leaving you bewildered by the roadside.

I suggest that you take a period of five weeks to begin to instigate a few changes. Just a few changes will make a huge difference. I recommend that:

- You look at your diet for the week (use the blank chart provided to help you to track your eating habits over the week).
- Re-work your diet and ensure that your plate has the following ratio, 40% carbohydrates, 40% protein, 20% healthy fats (such as avocados and nuts). (Use the blank charts to write in your new dietary changes). Make a note of how you feel with the changes: what was difficult for you, what was easy for you to do, how you feel.
- Every week incorporate some of the principles from the beginning of the chapter: Creating the Right Food Essence. A good principle to incorporate first is the "do not eat after 6pm". Then "do not overeat". You will feel a big difference by just putting these two things into practice.
- See which supplements are missing from your diet. Try and incorporate them through making further dietary changes, drinking natural juices and where necessary supplementation.

Five Week Review

Food I have eaten for the week

Day & Date	FOOD	QTY	Time eaten	Made at	Eaten at

Change For The Week: Worksheet 1

	Food item/s	Eating Habits	Review
Day 1			
Day 2			
Day 3			
Day 4			
Day 5			
Day 6			
Day 7			

Change For The Week: Worksheet 2

	Food item/s	Eating Habits	Review
Day 1			
Day 2			
Day 3			
Day 4			
Day 5			
Day 6			
Day 7			

Change For The Week: Worksheet 3

	Food item/s	Eating Habits	Review
Day 1			
Day 2			
Day 3			
Day 4			
Day 5			
Day 6			
Day 7			

Change For The Week: Worksheet 4

	Food item/s	Eating Habits	Review
Day 1			
Day 2			
Day 3			
Day 4			
Day 5			
Day 6			
Day 7			

Change For The Week: Worksheet 5

	Food item/s	Eating Habits	Review
Day 1			
Day 2			
Day 3			
Day 4			
Day 5			
Day 6			
Day 7			

Journey pages

The best way out is always through
ROBERT FROST

Journey pages

Principle 6: Awaken the Mind-Body Type

Trust that still, small voice that says,
"this might work and I'll try it."

DIANE MARIECHILD

Earth, Wind, Fire, and Water

As you have journeyed towards self mastery you have learned about the soul; how to move through your fear and pain; how to hear the messages of your inner self; ways nourish the mind, body and spirit. Now is a good time to learn about your unique mind-body type. The concept of a unique mind-body type is important to all traditional Asian systems. In Ayurvedic medicine knowing it is crucial to helping you maintain balance in your life.

At birth we are all born with an energy type which we inherit from our father and mother. Our individual energy type determines our personality, thought patterns, activities, foods, careers, diseases we will tend to be affected by during our life time. There were originally seven traditional universal mind-body types. Latter three more combinations were added.

Each mind-body type is created from a combination of the fundamental elements of life: space, air, fire, water, earth. They combine to form the three main bio energies of the body and life: Vata, Pitta and Kapha. In turn these three energy types combine to create the ten universal body types. The bio energies of life had been mentioned in the previous Principle. But it is worth briefly re-capping them. Vata is a combination of the element of space and air. It is likened to the wind and governs all movement in life. Pitta is created from fire and water. It is symbolized by fire and is in charge of all of life's metabolic actions. While Kapha is a combination of earth and water. It is like the earth and ensures the cohesion, structure and integrity of the body.

There are three single individual energy types but they are rare. Most of us are a dual energy type. This means that all the primordial energies of life constitute who we are with two being the most dominant and influential on our mind-body system. One of the two lead the way.

Body types

Type	Element	More information
Rare Body Type		
Vata	air/space	
Pitta	fire/water	
Kapha	water/earth	
Sama	balance of all three doshas	
Dual (original classification)		
Vata/Pitta	air/space main	fire/water subordinate
Vata/Kapha	air/space main	water/earth subordinate
Pitta/Kapha	fire/water main	water/earth subordinate
Additional Dual Body Type (contemporary classification)		
Pitta/Vata	fire/water main	air/space subordinate
Kapha/Vata	water/earth main	air/space subordinate
Kapha/Pitta	water/earth main	fire/water

Your Body Type

Each body type has its own tendencies and characteristics. Fill in The Mind – Body Type Quiz and discover what your unique mind-body type is. Note that you are a combination of all the doshas (energies) but two will predominate your special make – up. The lead energy of the two will have the greatest influence. For more information on your mind – body type read the descriptive charts for your lead energy and then the combination charts for the further flavour it adds to you. When most people find out their unique mind – body type they always seem to say, "That sounds just like me!"

MIND-BODY TYPE QUIZZ

Discover your unique mind-body type. You are combination of all three types: Vata, Pitta, and Kapha. However, it is the first two energy types with the highest number in the quiz that will form your unique mind-body type. The energy type with the very highest number has the greatest effect on you and it is said to be your lead energy. Answer all questions by circling the response that sounds the most like you. For each column count your ticks up and discover your mind – body type. So if you have the following ticks: Vata 6, Pitta 5, Kapha 3. You are a Vata Pitta type with Vata being your lead energy.

	Vata	Pitta	Kapha
Eyes	My eyes are small and alert.	My eyes are medium and penetrating.	My eyes are large and dreamy.
Complexion	My skin is dry, rough or thin.	My skin is reddish, prone to being irritated or blackheads.	My skin is soft and smooth.
Nails	My nails are thin and brittle.	My nails are having a red undertone.	My nails are strong and square.
Hair	My hair is thin, rough, and dry.	My hair is curly or fine with a tendency towards early graying.	My hair is thick, curly, wavy and luscious.
Weight	I tend to be slim and find it hard to put on weight.	I tend to always maintain a steady weight.	I tend to gain weight easily and find it hard to lose.
Frame	I have a thin, lanky frame with protruding joints.	I have a medium well built, muscular frame.	I have a large, round, stocky, broad frame.
Joints.	My joints are protruding and tend to crack.	My joints are flexible.	My joints are thick and well padded.
Temperament	I tend to be creative, full of ideas, and love change.	I am purposeful, active, highly motivated, and love to lead.	I am laid back, and don't mind being in the supportive role.
Learning	I tend to learn information quickly. I tend to also forget it quickly.	I learn quickly and like to see things through to the end.	I tend to learn information slowly but once I have learned something I retain it for well.
Sleep	I am a light sleeper and find it hard to fall asleep.	I tend to feel refreshed with less than eight hours of sleep.	I love to sleep and find it hard to wake up in the mornings.
Digestion	I tend to have irregular eating habits. When I eat I sometimes have indigestion and bloating after meals.	I tend to have a strong healthy appetite. Often I feel hungry soon after eating.	I tend to feel heavy after eating.
Body	I tend to have cold hands and feet.	I tend to feel warm in all	I tend to like all

Temperature	I love warm climates.	seasons and prefer cool temperatures.	climates but hate cold, wet days.
Stress	I tend to feel anxious and worry a lot when under stress.	I tend to feel irritated and aggressive under stress.	I tend to withdraw and stop socializing under stress.
Write no. of checks			

I am Vata, I Rush Like the Wind

General attributes	Light, dry, mobile, rough, cold, thin, clear.
Frame	I tend to be thin, tall or short with physical irregularities
Weight	I find it hard to gain weight and easy to lose
Shape of face	I have a thin, long, egg shaped, small forehead
Skin	My skin tends to be dry, sallow looking with small pores. It tends to premature wrinkles, dark circles under my eyes and I tan very easily.
Hair	My hair is dry, frizzy and thin. I have been told that some Vata people also have very coarse hair.
Nails	My nails tend to be brittle.
Eyes	My eyes are small.
Appetite	I do not like to eat regularly as I hate routine.
Stamina	I get tired very easily.
Elimination	I suffer from regular constipation.
Sleep	I am a light sleeper.
Temperament	I tend to be fearful, indecisive, nervous, and anxious, worried and have a low tolerance.
lifestyle	I love being on the go, starting new creative projects and tossing ideas around.
Good qualities	I am a very accommodating, active, creative, intelligent, natural teacher, musician, spiritual leader, artists, and philosopher.
sexuality	I am very variable in my taste and love the idea of love more than the actual act of love.
Prone to	I seem to be prone excessive dryness, dry eczema, dry skin conditions, dandruff, wrinkles, irritable bowel syndrome, constipation, sharp pains, backaches, nervous disorders, insomnia, bone problems, arthritis, anxiety, fatigue, sleeping disorders.

I am Kapha, Stable Like Earth

General attributes	heavy, cool, damp, oil, sweet, dense.
Frame	I tend to be broad, well built and evenly proportioned.
Weight	I gain weight easily and find it hard to lose.
Shape of face	My face is round but I have noticed there are some Kapha types who have square faces.
Skin	My skin is cool, oily with large pores. It is prone to black heads, cystic acne, scarring, deep wrinkles, and getting sun tanned.
Hair	My hair is thick, curly, shiny, oily and black.
Nails	My nails are clear, pale, square and white.
Eyes	People say my eyes are sensual and dreamy.
Appetite	I love to eat, especially for comfort. I love sweet creamy things, cake, and anything made with flour.
Stamina	I tend to have a strong good immune system.
Elimination	My elimination is slow, regular and moderate.
Sleep	I love to sleep.
Temperament	I am easily depressed, prone to laziness, stubbornness, get attached to things and I can be possessive.
lifestyle	I tend to be easy going and do not like too much change in my routine.
Good qualities	I tend to be calm, stable, dependable, nurturing, good memory, good provider, artists, dancer, doctor, accountant, teacher and parent.
sexuality	I am warm, nurturing, a good lover, romantic and have a lot of stamina.
Prone to	I seem to be prone to headaches, sore throats, respiratory problems, swellings, asthma, tumors, fibroids, acne, wet eczema, memory issues, learning difficulties, weight gain, water retention, edema, diabetes, sinus problems, depression, lethargy, and edema.

I am Pitta, hot like fire

General attributes	Hot, sharp, slightly oily, sour, light fluid.
Frame	I tend to have a medium and proportioned frame.
Weight	I tend to gain weight easily and lose it easily.
Shape of face	I have a triangular shape face with a pointed chin.
Skin	I have warm, soft, reddish skin with large pores in the T-zone. My skin tends to be prone to allergic reactions.
Hair	My hair is soft, straight, light or reddish, Premature gray.
Nails	My nails are soft, pink and well formed.
Eyes	My eyes are almond shaped.
Appetite	I tend to get hungry easily, and very thirsty.
Stamina	I am moderate in strength.
Elimination	My stools tend to be loose, regular and large.
Sleep	I don't sleep a lot. When I sleep it is very sound.
Temperament	I must admit, I am prone to anger, frustration, jealousy, aggressive and sometimes irritability.
lifestyle	I love doing things where I can be the leader.
Good qualities	I tend to be adaptable, ambitious, sensitive, compassionate, sharp, intelligent, a good business person, administrator, director and pioneer.
sexuality	I am intense and sometimes impatient.
Prone to	I seem to be prone to acne, rashes, cold sores, allergic reactions, burning sensations, blood disorders, peptic ulcers, boils, anger, bleeding of the liver, hypertension and falling hair.

Combinations

Vata-Pitta (read for Pitta/Vata)

You have all the characteristics of Vata. You are creative, erratic, a great intellectual and hate routine. You also love warmth because of your cold energy. However Pitta adds an interesting slant to your personality type. Although you enjoy cold weather you definitely have a limit to the amount of heat you can tolerate. You have the fear of Vata and the anger of Pitta which alternates frequently.

At your most balanced you have a great capacity for original thought and Pitta's ability to apply it. On a downside you have a tendency towards addictive behavior because of Vata's tendency to avoid pain and Pitta's gravitational pull towards addiction. You can also tend to be arrogant and need the stability of the earth element to ground you more.

Vata-Kapha (read for Kapha - Vata)

You have all the characteristics of your lead energy Vata. However with a Kapha influence you have an interesting twist going on. Both Vata and Kapha are united in their coldness. So there is a even deeper need for warmth and comfort. You will also tend to have a sluggish and slow digestive system. Vata makes you a zealous personality in all that you do, combined with the persistence of Kapha this trait is doubled. Vata is a cool energy which needs a lot of warmth, Kapha too. So emotions and emotional hurt swirls around at a much deeper level than most mind-body energy types. You may tend to look for love in all the wrong places. You need the element of fire to help you feel more integrated.

Pitta-Kapha (read for Kapha/Pitta)

You have all the characteristics of your lead energy Pitta which gives you the ability to deal with constant change. It also gives you ambition while Kapha imbues you with stability making you a successful and rounded personality type. With Pitta you will tend towards anger but you are in luck – Kapha's cool nature tapers your temper calming it down quickly. However, on a downside Pitta tends towards arrogance and Kapha towards surety. The result – a kind off smug arrogance. Because the spirituality Vata is minimized in your mind-body type you need to incorporate more spiritual practice into your life to help you live a life of balance.

Body Type in Balance

Your body type has certain foods, lifestyle and emotions that keeps it in balance. See the charts below to figure out what they are:

Vata :Lifestyle Chart

Vata	
Vegetables	
Favour or include	Artichokes, asparagus, beets, carrots, cucumber, garlic, cooked, green beans, okra, onions, cooked food, radishes, sweet potatoes, turnips, watercress, yams.
Avoid or Reduce	Broccoli, Brussels, sprouts, cabbage, cauliflower, celery, eggplant, leafy green vegetables, mushrooms, potatoes, sprouts. If you have them cook them with oil which soothes the dryness.
Fruits	
Favour or Include	Apricots, avocados, bananas, cherries, coconut, dates, figs, grapes, lemons, limes, mangoes, melons, nectarines, oranges, papayas, peaches, pineapple, plums, raspberries, stewed fruits, strawberries.
Avoid or Reduce	Apples (green), cranberries, pears, pomegranates, dried fruits, and unripe fruit.
Grains	
Favour or Include	Basmati rice, cooked oats, couscous, mung dhal, rice, wheat.
Avoid or Reduce	Barley, buckwheat, corn, dry oats, lentils, millet.
Dairy	
Favour or Include	All dairy is acceptable.
Avoid or Reduce	
Meats	
Favour or Include	Chicken, eggs, fish, turkey.
Avoid or Reduce	All red meat (beef, lamb, pork, venison, etc).
Oils	
Favour or Includes	Sesame oil, but all oils are acceptable.
Avoid or Reduce	
Sweeteners	
Favour or Include	Cane sugar, honey, molasses, maple syrup, but all natural sweets are acceptable.
Avoid and Include	Refined sugars, artificial sweetener.
Nuts & Seeds	
Favour or Include	Almonds, but all nuts and seeds are acceptable in small amounts.

Avoid or Reduce	
Spices	
Favour or Include	Almost all spices are acceptable in moderation, with emphasis on sweet and heating herbs and spices: all spice, anise, basil, bay leaf, black pepper, caraway, cardamom, cilantro, cinnamon, dove, cumin, fennel, ginger, horseradish, juniper berries, liquorice root, mace, marjoram, mustard, nutmeg, oregano, sage, sea salt, tarragon, thyme.
Beverages	
Favour or Include	All fruit juices, spice teas, warm milk, warm water.
Avoid or Reduce	All fizzy and carbonated drinks.
Lifestyle	
Favour or Include	Cool calming activities, gentle exercises, meditation, and routine, confident.
Avoid or Reduce	Hectic activity, over work, and erratic behavior, skipping meals.

Pitta Lifestyle Chart

Pitta	
Vegetables	
Favour or include	Asparagus, broccoli, Brussels sprouts, cabbage, cauliflower, celery, courgettes, cucumber, green beans, leafy greens, lettuce, mushrooms, okra, peas, potatoes, sprouts, sweet potatoes.
Avoid or Reduce	Aubergines, beets, carrots, garlic, hot peppers, onions, parsnips, radishes, spinach, tomatoes.
Fruits	
Favour or Include	Fruits should be sweet and ripe. Apples, avocados, cherries, dates, figs, red grapes, (not sour), mangoes, melons, oranges (not sour), pears, pineapple, (not sour), plums, pomegranates, prunes, raisins.
Avoid or Reduce	Apricots, berries, cherries (sour), grapefruit, papayas, persimmons.
Grains	
Favour or Include	Barley, Basmati rice, oats, wheat, wheat rice.
Avoid or Reduce	Brown rice, corn, millet, rye.
Dairy	
Favour or Include	Butter, cottage cheese, cream, egg whites, ghee, ice cream, milk.
Avoid or Reduce	
Meats	
Favour or Include	Chicken, shrimp, turkey.
Avoid or Reduce	All red meat such as beef, pork, lamb, etc. and seafood.
Oils	
Favour or Includes	only in small amounts – canola, coconut oil, olive oil, sunflower oil.
Avoid or Reduce	
Sweeteners	
Favour or Include	All natural sweeteners, except honey and molasses.
Avoid and Include	All artificial sweeteners.
Nuts & Seeds	
Favour or Include	Almonds, cashews, coconuts, pumpkin seeds, sunflower seeds..

Avoid or Reduce	All other nut and seeds.
Spices	
Favour or Include	Sweet, bitter and astringent spices are acceptable in small amounts – basil, cardamom, coriander, leaves and seeds, dill, fennel, mint, nutmeg, saffron, turmeric.
Beverages	
Favour or Include	Alfalfa teas, comfrey tea, cool water, dandelion tea, hibiscus tea, mint tea, sweet juices.
Avoid or Reduce	Warming teas and beverages.
Lifestyle	
Favour or Include	cool activities, meditation, spiritual activities.
Avoid or Reduce	Too much of a hectic lifestyle and slow down.

Kapha Lifestyle Chart

Kapha	
Vegetables	
Favour or include	Green peppers, leafy greens, lettuce, mushrooms, okra, onions, peas, peppers, potatoes, radishes, spinach, sprouts, squash, watercress.
Avoid or Reduce	Sweet and juicy – courgettes, cucumbers, sweet potatoes, tomatoes.
Fruits	
Favour or Include	Apples, apricots, cranberries, grapefruit, kiwi, pears, persimmons, pomegranates, dried fruits.
Avoid or Reduce	Sweet, sour or very juicy fruit. Avocados, bananas, dates, fresh figs, grapefruit, grapes, mangoes, melons, oranges, papayas, peaches, pineapples, plums.
Grains	
Favour or Include	Barley, Basmati rice, buckwheat, corn, millet, rye.
Avoid or Reduce	Hot cereals and steamed grains-oats, wheat (except small amounts).
Dairy	
Favour or Include	Minimize all dairy products.
Avoid or Reduce	
Meats	
Favour or Include	Chicken, shrimp, turkey.
Avoid or Reduce	All red meat like, beef, pork, lamb and seafood.
Oils	
Favour or Includes	Almond oil, corn oil, mustard oil, safflower oil, sunflower oil.
Avoid or Reduce	
Sweeteners	
Favour or Include	Raw, unheated honey may be used as a sweetener.
Avoid and Include	All other sweeteners.
Nuts & Seeds	
Favour or Include	In small amounts – almond, sunflower, pine nuts.
Avoid or Reduce	All other nut and seeds
Spices	
Favour or Include	Almost all spices may be eaten.
Beverages	
Favour or Include	Cinnamon tea, clove tea, dandelion tea, ginger tea, vegetable juices, warm water.
Lifestyle	

Favour or Include	More activity, vigorous exercise, socializing more,
Avoid or Reduce	Laziness, over eating, and being alone.

Your Body Imbalance

You have learned that you have a mind-body type. You have also learned how to keep it in balance. The cool thing is that it is also easy to holistically manage an illness by following the mind – body type guidelines. So Imagine you have arthritis. How do you deal with it using the mind-body information provided within these pages? Simple. Just follow the guidelines below:

1. Locate the mind-body type charts which contain information on which type of illness belongs to which mind-body type. These charts are entitled: *I am Vata, I Rush Like the Wind, I am Kapha, Stable Like Earth, I am Pitta, Hot Like Fire* charts. You will notice that your imaginary arthritis condition falls under the *I am Vata I Rush Like the Wind* chart. You will notice that chart also contains information on the Vata mind-body characteristics. Note, that when you have an illness or condition you will manifest many of the mind-body type traits of the body type it falls within. So don't skip over reading about the traits of that type.
2. Now go to the *Vata Life Style Chart.* This will help you to know which foods you should include or extract from your diet. It will also inform you of other lifestyle choices appropriate for the mind-body type you are dealing with. Know that just making a few changes at a time from this chart reaps huge benefits.
3. Now it's time to go to *Principle 4: Awaken Body Bliss.* Follow the appropriate *Seasonal Balancing Routine Chart* for the mind-body type you are dealing with. So your imaginary arthritis will benefit from following the *Vata Seasonal Balancing Routine Chart*; along with the other general recommendations provided.

Journey pages

The soul doesn't necessarily benefit from long,
hard work, or from fairness of any kind.
Its effects are achieved more with magic than effort.
THOMAS MOORE

Principle 7: Awaken Sacred Balance

*The earth has received the embrace
of the sun and we shall see the results
of that love. He put in your heart certain
wishes and plans; in my heart, he put
other different desires.*

CHIEF SITTING BULL

The Circle of Wisdom

Many centuries ago men and women sat in awe under the starry night sky and observed it. Drawn in by how its grandeur spread its wings languidly from one corner of their world to another. Is it surprising that they were overcome with a feeling that there was something so much greater than themselves and filled with the over whelming question "who am I in relation to all of this?" It is a question that would echo down the hallowed hallways of generations, cultures and worlds.

Under the blinking sky the gazing eyes of those men and women would have noticed that under the stillness of the night sky was a throbbing movement of order. One that crops and heart beats danced in harmony with.

It might have been in moments like those mentioned that the Aborigines, Egyptians, Babylonians, Native American Indians realized that we are all part of a circle of wisdom where we are one, share the same universal soul and operate on the same principles of universal existence. The Aborigines saw visions of Dreamtime. They heard its whispers wandering through the heartbeat of stories, songs, rites and sacred places. For they say it is within the Dreamtime that life arose and all the principles that govern it. Here spirits came to earth, and chose their form as plant, animal or human making an everlasting pact, "each one will look after the other". It is from the sacred elements and the pool of consciousness from which we emerged and we draw our strength. It is from being at one with the elements that we maintain our sense of sacred balance.

The Lake of Forgetfulness

If "each one will look after the other" and recognize their connection to each other was the pact made at the time. It seems that time has a way of fading the memory. For excitedly, in a different time, in the corridor of the inquisitive mind, the Greeks asked the same question "who am I?". It was one that led them to begin the separation of science "the knowledge of knowing" from the metaphysical. As the form of nature began to dazzle the beholders mind the science of deductive and inductive reasoning began the arduous passage of pushing its head out of the mother's womb. Now it became the mystery of the pieces of the whole over the whole that preoccupied the heart and mind of man.

It was the loud echo of the English physicist Sir Isaac Newton (1642-1727) that announced once and for all that we are separate from nature. A song that danced at the welcoming entrance of the Age of Enlightenment where German philosopher Immanuel

Kant (1724-1804) took God completely out of the scientific equation. Reality could now be measured in a mechanical way, through math, through anything other than the dance of the Soul meeting the Soul.

Millions of years of evolution were brushed aside with the sleight of the hand. The ancient pact now parceled away in a box made for everything marked as "nonsensical" and "primitive". The advancement into the Darwinian Age saw the split between science and the metaphysical world deepen. The Age was heralded in by British Naturalist Charles Darwin (1809-1882) who wrote *On the Origin of the Species by Means of Natural Selection*, or the *Preservation of Favored Races in the Struggle for Life*. The shaky platform for the advancement of Industrialism, greed, corruption, a dangerous disregard for Mother Earth and each other was set – as David Landes author of *The Wealth and Poverty of Nations* helps us to understand.

The Dreamtime Awakens

The memory of the pact may have faded but the fact that we are an integral part of "The Everything" is the enduring reality written on faces of rocks, in ice, on the telling rings of trees, and in the Egyptian arms of light that extend affectionately down from the sun. We are part of space, air, water and earth. We live and breathe these elements. From the cosmic consciousness they emerged to create all things, including us.

Twenty billion years ago is a hard time to imagine but the corridors of nature have shown that is when we may have begun. In a small dot of matter in the universe all the stuff of life was concentrated. Exploding grandly outward it hurtled dust clouds of life.

The clouds of dust clumped together and evolved into stars which in turn formed galaxies containing billions of their brothers and sisters. A beautiful mesmerizing galaxy with a tantalizing spiral body formed. On its outer skirts began the formation of a star which made all of life on earth possible – the sun. The sun was to capture our imagination from that day forward. From the dust clouds everything was formed including us.

Over eons the planet cooled down, the surface of the earth became covered with water and 2 billion years ago a small life form began - the Cynobacteria. It began the process of making food from sunlight with the help of the H_2O molecule (water). Today we call this process photosynthesis. It is essential to all life even today. Organisms that cannot engage in photosynthesis eat those that can. In effect we are all eating the energy of sunlight. We are made up of a grand total of 60 trillion cells; each one contains organelles which are descendants of these ancient bacteria which entered our cells.

"Who am I in this grand scheme of things?" is the question that plagued Einstein's mind. A mind that was on the constant search to discover what the "Old One" had intended.

The answer emerged from the whirling tides of his soul. Like a golden fish coming up for air came forth the formula E=MC2 – energy forms matter and matter goes back to energy (the nutshell explanation).

In the Saturday Evening Post, October 26th 1929 Einstein gives us an insight into the songs of the Dreamtime that plagued his soul, "we are in the position of a little child entering a huge library, whose walls are covered to the ceiling with books in many different languages. The child knows someone must have written those books. It does not know who or how. It does not understand the language in which they are written. The child notes a definite plan in the arrangement of the books, a mysterious order, which it does not comprehend but only dimly suspects."

It's hard to keep the song of Dreamtime down. British Physicists David Bohm (1917-1992) agreed with Einstein's vision of the "Old One". He came to a clarifying realization that the universe is "an undivided and unbroken whole". The "whole" was the hidden primary reality (the quantum potential) that provides information to the totality of humankind and its environment.

Sacred Elements

We are the space, air, fire, water and earth. The ancients told us that each of these elements make up life. They are our Mothers. Just look at Obatala's Ladder, the West African story which shows us the unfolding ladder of DNA and the elements descending from the sky or the Dance of Leela in the Indian story of the beginning of life. Is it the truth of these connections that played on Yoga Master BKS Iyengar mind as he wrote in the *Light on Life*, "Just as we cannot separate the element of earth from the sheath of our physical body, so we cannot separate space from the blissful sheath. In asana (posture) we are playing with the elements. When we twist, for example, we are squeezing space out of the kidney, and on release, space returns, and space becomes renewed. Similarly, we are squeezing water, fire, air, as well as to some extent earth, out of an organ when we twist or contract. When we release, circulation comes back, restoring revitalized elements. We think of this as washing and cleansing the organs. This is true on an elemental level. What we are doing is playing with the balance of the elements, experiencing which sensation each will bring us."

On the most fundamental level we can see that we reflect our Mother Earth. For we are 70% water and so is she. When she breathes out we breathe in the very substance exhaled, oxygen. When we breathe out others in our biosphere breathe in our exhalation, Carbon dioxide. So the dance goes on over and over again.

The Long Farewell

Why should we care about our place in the world? Why should we care about the fact we are part of everything? Maybe one reason is to avoid what Jonathan Weiner, author of *Planet Earth* called in the last chapter of his book the "Long Farewell". He poetically shares,

"But the farewell is now before us. We are living it. Our dreams are troubled by the bomb and by the rocket. We are the generation in the doorway. We are the first generation of the long good-bye. As we look around today, we see sky, hills, peaks, and waves with a peculiar attention. We stare, as if we were already looking back. This is the planet on which our species grew up. This is the planet from which, with luck, we will step toward the stars. If we survive, and make it up there, it will be because we have acquired a new measure of wisdom, and perhaps by then we will be worthy of the long cosmic trip."

Or maybe it is because we need to care about the fact we are on a rapid "melt down". In the March 2009 issue of Merco Press, amongst various other National publications stated clearly we are living in a melting reality, "last month, scientists contributing to the UN Polar Year survey said ice caps on both poles are melting at a much faster pace than expected. A Polar Year statement said researchers found Arctic ice levels at their lowest point since satellites began measuring the northern ice mass three decades ago."

Then there is the reality that we cannot move to planet Mars. Besides the fact that the mighty red planet is totally inhabitable to us. Even if it was habitable, imagine what we would do to it? How would we inhabit a new planet? According to research paper *Ecosystem Services: Benefits Supplied to Human Societies by Natural Ecosystems* written by up to eleven environmental scientists and published in the Ecological Society of America 1997. If we even found a planet that could sustain life we would have to think which species to take. Then that is only the beginning – we would have to work out which species were needed to support the primary ones. That includes: "the bacteria, fungi and invertebrates that help make soil fertile and break down wastes and organic matter; the insects, bats and birds that pollinate flowers; the grasses, herbs and trees that hold soil in place, regulate water cycle and supply food for animals". Then to just maintain soil alone we would need about "50,000 insects and mites, and nearly 50,000 algae, 400,000 fungi and billions of individual bacteria."

The Gift of the Mother Elements

As a young boy Martin Grey had remarkable inner visions. These visions made him yearn to be "a paintbrush in the hand of God". Then one day he picked up the National Geographic magazine and dreamed of becoming an explorer and photographer in exotic lands. At the age of twelve his father took his family to India for four years. In that time he became allured by even further visions. Then one day he thought of producing a photography book of great Asian pilgrimage shrines. On returning to the States he entered the University of Arizona and began to study archeology. But his childhood visions would not go away. They lured him into spending ten years as a monk in both India and Asia. But there was something else to his visions that kept on pulling him. It was a "something else" that would not go away. It was the "something else" that he had dreamed of when he was younger and had him one day he on his bike and begin a twenty-year period of traveling as a wandering pilgrim to more than one thousand sacred sites in eighty countries around the world.

What did Grey learn during his remarkable journey? He discovered that the deities across the world were always associated with specific places. These deities mirrored the feminine or masculine energy of various sacred spots. Their stories and images also embodied a commentary of the power of those sacred places and the elements that made them up. Grey believes that it is beneficial for individuals to make pilgrimages to those sites because of their transformational energy. "These legendary places have a mysterious capacity to awaken and catalyze within visitors the qualities of compassion, wisdom, peace of mind, and respect for the earth". Grey believes that the increasing of these qualities is vital in consideration of the numerous ecological and social problems that occur in the world.

As a result of my own journey with water, ecology and healing I can personally vouch for what Grey is saying. In 2007 I began to experience intense dreams about fish dying, water being in trouble and the need to do something about it all. I received further visions and messages which were checked by a well respected West African priest. I was told that the Goddess of Water was giving me a calling to help heal the planet. Soon afterward I received an ancient title Crown of The Mother. The first thing I had to do as part of my role was to "go to water". I followed this instruction while I wondered "how could this help heal the world?"

During a period of two years I started the Humanity4Water project, visited rivers in the Caribbean, African and the United States. I worked alongside many Native American Nations (along with those from other communities) and became exposed to many sacred sites. I discovered that with each river visit I seemed to be more compassionate, thoughtful, aware and contemplative about the world. I received many dreams and much wisdom that guided me into a rich and rewarding spiritual journey. I went from being someone who was only partially aware of the world's problems to being someone who felt the pain of every insect, bird, tree, animal and person – literally! My desire to heal myself, my family and the world deepened. The same thing happened to my husband, mother and son. They all made the same journey and had similar experiences. During this period I also wrote *Dreamtime Awakening: A Journey With Mother Earth.* While my thirteen-year-old son wrote *The Chronicles of Endangered Animals*. His childhood love and compassion for animals increased.

We can all gain greater strength and increased power from a deeper connection to nature and the universe. Through learning about chakras we discovered how each element relates to our personalities and soul potential. We also discovered how to tap into the elements through breath work. By visiting power places, sacred sites and natural locations we can further tap into the Power of E (elements). Increasing our awareness also helps us to deepen our relationship with Mother Earth, Self and Each other. Now let's examine each element a little closer.

The Element of Water

As I washed my face in the water of the sacred Osun river that runs Southward through the ancient Yoruba lands of South Western Nigeria, I wondered about the many thousands before me who came day after day, month after month, year after year to supplicate the river with their prayers, silence, songs and awe.

It was June 2008 and I was staying with elders whose lives were intricately tied to the mighty heart beat of the river. When I was not staring into its waters I journeyed, with my husband and travel companions, over bumpy dirt roads and became an eye witness to dried rivers, wells running low, hunger, garbage piled high for lack of infrastructure, children forlorn yet full of hope, water too dirty to drink, human suffering painted onto a canvas of our own making.

After each trip, I entered the embrace of my abode, nestled close to the Osun Grove marked as a World Heritage Site. I was steeped in hundreds of years of history and a rhythm that seemed older than time itself. It was through the Grove the river flowed and where I, after a day's trip, washed the sorrow from my face.

My sighs echoed like the crew of Apollo 8, 1968, who saw the form of Mother Earth reveal her fragility as she rose above the lunar cycle. Commander Frank Borman later wrote, "it was the most beautiful, heart-catching sight of my life, one that sent a torrent of nostalgia, of sheer homesickness, surging through me. It was the only thing in space that had any color to it. Everything else was either black or white, but not the Earth." The "Earthrise" photo inspired the fledgling environmental movement. Its capturing of the sheer fragility of Mother Earth generated such love and respect for the planet. A year later after its release saw the first Earth Day and groundbreaking new laws.

"The perspective expanded again, to embrace all life in the universe, and all time since the creation," commented Robert Poole, author of *Earthrise: How Man First Saw the Earth*.

We are part of life's fragility. We are 70% water; the earth is 70% water too. We mirror the soul of our blue planet and the depths of its blue oceans in whose watery world ancient bacteria found a miraculous way to capture the sun and use its energy giving back another gift – one of oxygen. Our 60 trillion cells contain organelles, which contain these ancient bacteria. Our breath is the oceans breath. For it provides us with 50% of our oxygen we need to stay alive. What appears to be still waters is a torrent of vibrant moving life. The depths of our waters are not dead as proclaimed in 1841 by scientist Edward Forbes who dredged up 230 fathoms of sea in the Easter Mediterranean (a fathom is 6 feet), and came up with nothing.

Water moves in a cycle which reflects the oldest shape of mankind – the infinite zero. It loops around in a ceaseless hydrologic cycle which nourishes our cells, crops, children, blood, trees, rivers, skies and the world underground. In this hydrologic cycle the sun generously heats the liquid water in the oceans and lakes causing them to gloriously rise and condense into clouds whose shapes children love to name. Once full the clouds open like a heavenly door allowing the rains to fall and wet the soils for new growth before sinking deep into the ground and finding their way back to the water sources on earth.

Through this endless and ceaseless cycle 100 million billion gallons of water a year are cycled. Without this cycle it is not hard to imagine why life on earth would not be possible.

It is no wonder that water has inspired generations. To capture her voluptuous body, nurturing, ability to civilize, provide abundance, infinite wisdom, within the image of the river Goddess Ganga, Osun and Guan Yin and others. Or to declare heartfelt poems to the Goddess who contains "the secrets of the world".

Seventeenth century Brahmin Indian poet found himself at the foot of the Ganges river appealing to the heart of the Goddess Ganga. His soul ached with love and rejection. He was a devout Hindu who fell in love with a beautiful Muslim girl. Their love for each other ushered in the disdain of his elders and his banishment from their social circles. He tried to convince them of the sacredness and universality of love. But his words fell onto death ears. In frustration he went to the Goddess Ganga and staring out over her deep blue waters was moved to write,

Come to you as a child to his mother.
I come as an orphan to you, moist with love.
I come without refuge to you, giver of sacred rest.
I come a fallen man to you, uplifter of all.
I come undone by disease to you, the perfect physician.
I come, my heart dry with thirst, to you, ocean of sweet wine.
Do with me as you please.

This was one of 52 poems he wrote and collectively referred to them as *Ganga-Lahiri* or *Waves of Ganga*.

Now instead of writing poems to the sacred element of water, being moved to give gratitude to it or to appeal to its heart beat for help - we find it more befitting to pay homage to this sacred element that has sustained us since the beginning of time with thoughtlessness and a lack of care. Instead of poetic words we create 260 million tonnes of plastic waste a year. And throw 10% of it into the oceans. With dire consequences to its rich ocean life. Its chemicals leak into the water creating a toxic soup. 44 percent of all marine birds eat the discarded plastic by mistake, while 267 marine species fall victim to its cancer producing chemicals. If we are not choking the river with plastic we are suffocating it with waste of some kind or another, building dams that break its spirit, and farming all its fish making the statistic of only 10 percent of the big fish in the ocean being alive a reality.

We don't have to defile this sacred element or any other we can tap into its power.

Earth

The fingers of winter caressed our faces. We stood there in the darkness on the even darker soil of the Catawba Indian Nation. The reservation was quiet as we bowed our heads in prayer. The immenseness of the night mingled with the flickering of five candles which which had been lit and floated on water in the simple humble gesture of gratitude for life on earth. We gave thanks for all that we had received from Mother Earth's waters and world. We also asked for our own healing, It was January 2009, the first water awareness and gratitude ceremony we at Humanity4Water conducted in South Carolina, United States.

Human history has been shaped from the richness of the earth's crust. Half a million years ago we were in the throes of the Stone Age where the stones of the earth shaped our existence. We then discovered that copper was easier to shape than stone taking us into the Copper Age. From the Copper Age we discovered how to separate iron from rock using heat heralding us into the Iron Age. From the 1750's we entered the Coal, Oil and Uranium Age. We have now near depleted the gifts provided by the sacred element of earth.

There is very little that we receive that we don't get from the earth: nourishment from the plants that grow towards the sun, oxygen from the outstretched trees and plant life that stretch elegantly upward toward the warm rays of the sun, a flourishing eco system, beauty that makes the eyes transfixed and the soul sing with joy.

The rainforest, the vital organs of the earth keep us going. Once they were twice the size of Europe, now they have been halved. They covered 14% of the world's surface now they spread their glory on only 6%. They are: 70 million years old; home to half of the world's species of 10 million plants, animals and insects; contain libraries of biodiversity; provide medicine for the world. Currently 25 % of the world's pharmaceutical cures come from the rain forest. The soil underneath the shade of the eye-catching branches of the great rainforest trees is not fertile as nutrients have been leached away after long periods of time. Now many of the roots of these trees reach upward absorbing their nutrients from the sky.

Yet, in our drive to whet the appetite of consumerism we clear these forests at 30 acres or more a minute. Much of the land is cleared to provide burgers for North Americans and for the profits of corporate companies.

The service of the rainforest, trees, animals, insects and plants that rise from the warmth of the soil is immense. Dig up one acre of soil beneath your feet and you may find bacteria, insects and soil life that is busy churning dead organic matter and waste into nutrients. You may well find: 50,000 small earthworms and their relatives, 50,000 insects and mites, nearly 12 million round worms, 30,000 protozoa, 50,000 algae, 400,000 fungi and billions of bacteria.

The soil itself does not stop yielding its service as it regulates our carbon, nitrogen and sulfur cycles and stores these contributions towards the warming of the planet deep in its robes.

These services and our relationship with the sacred element of earth has always been honored in the dances of the Cherokee as they dance to the Corn and Harvest Moons, the Ghanaians colorful sacred acknowledgment of the harvest season, as the Hindus give time worn praise in the Pongal Harvest festival. As Susan Griffin, Philosopher and Poet eloquently stated,

We know ourselves to be made from this earth.
We know this earth is made from our bodies.
For we see ourselves. And we are nature. We are nature seeing nature. We are nature with a concept
of nature. Nature speaking
of nature.

However, the advance of consumerism which was and is wrapped up in the words "advancement of civilization" has seen us break and ignore the sacred pact man has always had with the earth and earth with man. In times gone by we use to call Mother Earth by many names such as Aye, Panchama, Bunmi, Gaia - and in some places we still do. Our pact with her was treated as important to the survival of mankind and the whole of life by indigenous cultures across the corridors of the world. In the documentary *The Last Stand at Little Big Horn*, which addressed some of the myths surrounding "Custer's Last Stand", Sitting Bull epitomized the attitude of the "sacred pact" when he would not sell The Sacred Black Mountains. Disgusted he thought "what price can you put on the earth?" His disgust was echoed in his reply to the immigrant invaders who marched towards "progress", "We should take handfuls of the earth and sell it by the pound."

Fire

4th March 2009. It was the second Humanity4Water Water Awareness and Gratitude ceremony. The sound of flutes raised rhythmically into the air, enfolding ethereal fingers with the spirit of water , earth, air and the sun a dance so ancient that I stood there and enraptured the heart and soul. Thirty Native Americans from a variety of nations, those from other cultures swayed in time with the music as they offered up gratitude through prayers and song to the endless unconditional love and service of the sacred Healing Springs. A place which sprung from deep under the ground, connected to the long history of Blackville, South Carolina, and the Native Americans who healed families and wounded soldiers in its pristine pools.

This ceremony happened in the warmth and fire of the sun as so much of life has happened from the beginning of time. The gift of life is interesting and precious. It springs from the wells of water and the ability of plant life capture the energy of the sun turning it into turning it into building blocks and sustenance.

The Egyptians, Mayans, Aztecs, Bushmen, Dogons, Celts, and Gallic all watched the immeasurable power of the sun rise and fall. Keeping a note of where it rose in the sky and where it set. They carved monuments, planted stones like at the famous Nabta site of Sub Saharan Africa did breathtaking cave paintings which tracked the path of the sun.

The honoring of the sun can be seen in the oldest form of the Goddess in Egypt who wore the sun on her head representing the timeless union between mankind and this sacred element. It can be seen every day when the thousands gather at the banks of the Ganges River in India and await the large warm face of the sun, meeting it with songs, cheers and prayers. Rightfully, so. For we depend on this captivating star for the day, night, seasons, climates, food, warmth, oxygen we breath (which is replenished by photosynthesis), light, and for making our planet hospitable and livable. Formed 4.6 million years ago from the dust of one or more stars on the edge of our Milky Way galaxy the sun an ordinary star, is exceptional to us. As it lights up our whole world we may not think of the size of the sun. We get the true sense of its massiveness when we understand it is 93 million miles away from the earth. It is 745 times more massive than all the planets combined.

The signature for precious elements that make up life can be seen in the light of the sun as German Chemist Gustav Kirchhoff, and coworker Robert Bunsen discovered in 1859 as they examined the flame of a Bunsen burner. The sun and humans are made up of the same elements in the exact same quantity.

Space/Air

Somewhere and somehow, as I took up the baton of my calling and journeyed with water, I became aware of the sacred element of space and air It might have been somewhere between contemplating the magnetic essence of water, watching its meandering over obstacles or marveling at its infinite sparkles when the presence of space and air inched in to fill my awareness.

Space is the sacred element that fills our sphere of awareness quietly and without fanfare. It enters the pores of our daily activities unseen and unheard. Deep in its essence lies the mystery of the beginning of life that began with the Big Bang and the hurtling of life dust to all corners of its universe. Captivating the world in its universal chant of OM which flung open the eyes of all of life. As it breathlessly awoke life the Hindu ancients say that the element of air was born. To it all movement is assigned.

For it is air we first gulp in as we ease out from our mother's womb with fist raised in victory, and marvel in our eyes. We gasp as the life of air rushes, Prana, Chi, Vital Life Force and the life giving gas of oxygen through our blood. A ritual repeated in species across globes and worlds. 78% nitrogen and 21% oxygen air make up the matrix that we call air. Those who stared into the nights skies who wondered about the mysteries of life said it contained the breath of the creator itself. No wonder they believed this for it provides the gases that plants need for survival and the oxygen animals need for living.

Air is delicate. So delicate that small shifts can affect it drastically. Characterized by the beautiful, transformation energy of the Goddess Oya and God Vayu, air can mesmerize us with showers, mist, storms, floods and droughts. It is always moving, always restless as it does the stomp dance rising by day to the glory of the sun's warmth and falling by night as the sun begins to tuck away for sleep.

Love and Gratitude (They are elements as well!)

August 2009, my husband and I frantically prepared for the second Humanity4Water award ceremony. We did it from our own pockets, on very little money, but we were determined to honor those who like ourselves had decided to take the responsibility of being good planetary Stewards again. Sometimes, I wondered if we were crazy for doing a ceremony which was putting so much strain on us. But we were driven by the tremendous love we had for the rivers, all the sacred elements of life, our children, and humanity. We were also deeply moved by the love of those we were honoring, the ones who had dared to care and do something to secure the future of all generations.

Ultimately, I think the spirit of water taught me love and gratitude. The more I contemplated its gentle flow, its sustaining nature, its endless giving - was the more I seemed to contemplate the unconditional nature of love that seemed to ooze from the green pores of all living things and the gratitude that sustains that flow.

It was in the arms of Amma, known as a Universal Mother and Hugging Saint I experienced Love vs. love. In July 2009 my husband and I made our way to Washington on a stretched dollar to give Amma her Humanity4Water award in the area of Compassion. We were fortunate to be seated right next to Amma's light filled presence. Because of her devotion to healing through love and action she is known to hug thousands of people a day. She hugs the young, old, diseased, and well. I did not know that Love could transform so deeply until Amma enfolded me into her arms. The world went dark; it felt as though nothing else existed but the universe. In that hug my heart became fused with the unity of all things and filled with the gratitude that of of the immense blessing I felt.

As Amma said, "Love is our true essence. Love has no limitations of caste, religion, race or nationality. We are all beads strung together on the same thread of love"

So what is really this thing called love? In the West we see love as sexual and physical intimacy but author of *The Sacred Balance*, David Suzuki suggest that love is "a sacred element." From the time we are babies to the day we die we rely on the love and compassion of others. When a baby does not receive love it shows up as dense lines of x rays of the bones. The lines indicate periods when love was lacking and growth does not occur.

I remember reading an article in the Reader's Digest April 2008 edition. Learning to Love was the title that blazed in orange across the page. The small summary read, "seven years in a Romanian orphanage left Daniel Solomon broken and full of rage. How his new American family healed him and themselves". It was all topped of with a picture of the handsome face of a Romanian boy and the loving smile of his adoptive mother. My appetite was whetted enough for me to turn the page to discover the story behind the picture and title.

From the ages of 0 to five Daniel had spent his life in a Romanian orphanage. It was more like "a prison than a home for parentless children. Daniel was affectionate when he was adopted but he soon showed signs of severe behavior disorder as he "smashed toys and assaulted other kids". He was also committed to a psychiatric hospital.

What was behind Daniel's behavior? The article explains, "he had never owned a pair of shoes, never been read to, never gotten a hug. He didn't even know he had parents." If Heidi Solomon and her husband knew what they would be getting themselves into I wonder if they would have still adopted Daniel. But they did. Heidi says that at first his behavior was normal (despite a few tantrums). Then one day he turned eight and had a birthday party.

Instead of being a time of celebration it marked a long road of rage and fury as Daniel realized "someone had brought him into the world and abandoned him". Unfortunately, he believed that "someone" was his adoptive father and mother. Even though they tried to explain to him they weren't his biological parents his anger needed something to fix itself on and they became the "it" from childhood games.

They tried to help him as much they could. They bought him a puppy; he tried to strangle it. They took him to therapists; he bit a three-inch gash in the stomach of one. They sent him to a good school; he threatened his principal with a shard of glass. They gave him as much love as humanly possible; he head butted his mother, gave her a black eye and took a knife to her throat. Daniel not only loathed his new parents he loathed himself. He contemplated suicide many times.

According to psychotherapist Daniel was suffering from attachment-disorder. It simply means someone who believes they are bad, unwanted, worthless and unlovable. As a result, they are unable to receive or demonstrate love. While the disorder is rare it is commonly found in abused children, including the thousands adopted in the United States every year from "warehouse-style" Eastern European orphanages.

Most individuals would have abandoned Daniel out of frustration, washed their hands of him but Heidi and her husband did not. Their love kept them going, their knowledge that he needed love also kept them trying to find solutions. Institutions and drugs did not work. So Heidi decided she would try a different approach. There was a gentler way of healing according to Ronald Federici, a Virginia neuropsychologist. Albeit gentle it was very demanding. For two months solid Heidi and her husband had to stand three feet from Daniel. He was not to ask for anything but food and clothes. He had to maintain eye contact each and every time he asked for something. The therapy was based on re-creating the mother-baby bond they had never developed. A bond Daniel had never developed with anyone.

Daniel began to change and transform. He became more loving, appreciated how much his parents had done for him. Then to everyone's amazement Daniel received his synagogue award for most outstanding high school student. He then said three words to his parents he had never said before, "I love you".

Today Daniel is still in therapy, the lack of love he received in his life means he has great trouble reading and writing. He will not be able to go to college, but he now wants to give back the love he received and learned to recognize by becoming a fire man.

It is no wonder Bernie Siegal, surgeon and author commented in his book, *Peace, Love and Healing* – "the world would be a better place with love". The basis of his statement is rooted in the fact that the Pygmies of South Africa who demonstrate a lot of touching and affection have no crime, no infidelity, no stigma against sexuality and a great respect, "not only for each other, especially the elders amongst them, but for the forest in which they dwell."

His Holiness The fourteenth Dalai Lama Tenzin Gyatso of Tibet shares, "all phenomenon from the planet we inhabit to the oceans, clouds, forests, and flowers that surround us, arise independence upon subtle patterns of energy. Without their proper interaction they dissolve and decay." He further states it is this independence which results in our need and desire for love. As Amma shares, "there are two types of poverty in the world, financial poverty and poverty of love, the second is more important." As the second creates the first.

It would seem that David Suzuki, author of *The Sacred Balance* was right when he stated love is another element. However, I would like to add that I think Gratitude is also an element that helps sustain the nourishing flow of our world. Gratitude goes hand in hand with Love. In Daniel's story his love is accompanied by large measures of gratitude. It seems to be the vessel that allows his love to be expressed and grow. As my husband said, "I sincerely believe gratitude is love unveiled."

Healing Journey Exercise

You can live a life grounded by the Mother Elements and through them you can come home to yourself. Besides the exercises below, may we also ask the Mother Elements for their forgiveness, give them gratitude and send love their way.

1. Mother Water – connect with the clarifying and cleansing aspect of water by visiting her locations, such as a river, ocean, water fall, stream etc. Spend time reflecting on her nature, allow her wisdom and clearing flow to energetically heal your life. You can also visualize the Mother Water element in your meditations. You can see her as a blue or white flow of light, water, or as a gentle mother dressed in blue or white healing your life. You can bring her into your life through her joyful scents of ylang ylang, sweet orange, rose, tangerine, or Amber. Have something at home that represents water like a water fountain.

2. Mother Earth – connect with the grounding aspect of earth by taking a slow mindful walk in the park, go for a hike, do anything that allows you to be in contact with the earth element. Allow her wisdom nature to expand your feeling of joy, generosity and balance. You can visualize the Mother Earth Element in your meditations healing you. See her dressed in a flowing yellow dress, as a golden Earth Mother. You can ground yourself with her scents of vetiver, germanium and other earthy scents. Bring the grounding energy of earth to your home and life through stones you collect, crystals you treasure etc.

3. Mother Fire – connect with the energizing aspects of fire by going into places that are warm, where you can observe the sun and be one with her. Allow her energy of passion, positive perception and compassion to fill you up. You can visualize her in the meditative state as a beautiful vibrant woman dressed in red. Allow her to heal you and even give you a gift. Ground yourself with her tantalizing scents of bergamot, cedarwood, ylang ylang, orange and sandalwood. Light exotic and beautiful candles to bring Mother Fire element into your home.

4. Mother Air – connect with her expanding playful nature. Go to places where you can be touched by her energy. Allow her to heal you in your meditations. See her as a woman dressed in green or multi-colored. Is she still or twirling? Does she give you a gift? What is it? What is the message in the gift. Tap into her clearing nature through her scents of rosemary, sage, peppermint, lemon grass. Keep objects of Mother Air in your home – like feathers and wind-chimes.

5. Mother Space – she is the element we all rest within in allowing us to experience a feeling of spaciousness and peace in our lives See her in your meditation as a luminous light flowing over, in you, and helping you to release the things that are blocking. You can use clearing aromatherapy oils such as peppermint, sage, rosemary to tap into her restful energy.

House on The Sand

Imagine you spent time, money and lots of effort building your dream house. At the end of building it you feel proud in the midst of your sweat and tears. You look at the house from afar and admire its beauty. You walk through the house and love how it looks and feels. You wake up in the house and thank God for the blessing. Then one day the weatherman warns everyone in your neighborhood to prepare for an oncoming hurricane. It looks like it's on a collision course for your area but then again it may swerve by leaving it untouched. You panic a little and begin to get your house hurricane proof. "There is no way I am going to lose this beautiful house I have just built," you vow aloud to yourself. Especially after all the blood, sweat and tears you put into it.

The house we are speaking of, is of course your personal house that you have spent time getting into order. Time getting into sacred balance. In Yoga philosophy we are told that when we are building our personal house we must safe guard it. Safe guard it against what? And safe guard it how? We must safe guard it against the emotions and actions which will rob us of our new-found treasures in the dead of the night and even in the dead of the day. "Be aware," says the Yoga masters "of The Five Afflictions." Also make sure your house is built on the four essential pillars of life: dharma, artha, kama and moksha; and it has inbuilt into it the central pillars of Yama (ethics). "Tell me more," you gasp worrying about the oncoming hurricane. So they do.

The Five Afflictions

The Five Afflictions are known as: Ignorance, Arrogance, Attachment and Aversion and a Fear of Death. It is said Ignorance is the root of all the afflictions. Why? Because ignorance keeps us in the dark. It is the inability to know what is real. Real in Yoga philosophy and all ancient cultures is that which is "not perishable" and that which is "enduring". So the soul is not perishable. It is everlasting and therefore the true source of the happiness we hanker after in life. On the other hand the ego and all the things it aims to accumulate in life: money, wealth, material goods, prestige – are perishable. They do not last and therefore can never truly bring us true happiness. Wealth can go, material goods can go, prestige can go but the Soul cannot. Knowing this stands us in the all embracing and clarifying light of truth. Ignorance stands us in the dark; it turns our world upside down and puts us in a state of confusion as we chase all the wrong things, ideas and emotions. As Yoga Master and author BKS Iyengar states in the *Light on Life* "Ignorance is the Devil". The Devil of the West is clever and smart, and leads us into trouble to do evil acts. In Yogic traditions the Devil is the part of us that is far from smart. Far from all knowing. It is Ignorance itself and it is Ignorance that leads us into doing and committing small to large erroneous deeds.

Iyengar further states that the second affliction: Arrogance emerges directly from the first one. For when we judge ourselves to be anything other than our Universal Soul we get caught up in judging by externals and worthless comparisons. "Arrogance stems from pride which lies in difference, not in equality. You are pretty, but I am ugly. I am fierce, but you are weak. I own a house, but you are a beggar. I am right but you are wrong," Iyengar reveals.

But what about the third, fourth and fifth afflictions, Attachment, Aversion and Fear of Death? Iyenger points the finger once again right back to Ignorance. Attachment comes from ego which is attracted to possessing things and owning the world. Indulging in Attachment can only lead to misery. While Aversion is the opposite of Attachment. Aversion is based on superficiality. It is based on the likes and dislikes of our ego. The Soul is more merciful and kinder in its judgments than ego. It sees only the light and beauty of all things in life.

The Soul's understanding that nothing dies also brings us to the last affliction – Fear of Death. We live in a society where people spend millions on cosmetic surgery so that they can immortalize themselves. We live in a society where people are afraid of passing away. These fears keep us away from a peaceful mind and a deepened state of happiness. For we are always fearfully clinging onto things. We want to defeat the natural passing away of something: our jobs, our lives, the life of those we love? We become possessive about the people and things in our lives and why? Because we don't believe in the grandeur, everlastingness, and solidity of the Soul itself. Being fearful of things takes up so much energy. Instead of being afraid to have something pass through the tight grip of our hands why don't we release that same energy to live fully in the present moment?

Burmese painting of Indian Goddess Saraswati, Goddess of knowledge, music and arts

The Four Aims of Life

Before you take a deep breath, and before you relax remember you have not finished making your house hurricane proof. You need some strength to erect the Four Pillars of Life. For if that hurricane does hit your house it really cannot do much damage when the house has the Four Pillars of Life. They are the four things we really do in our everyday lives. So what are they? Dharma (doing your rightful duty), Artha (being self reliant through earning an income), Kama (Pleasure of love and human enjoyment), Moksha (freedom). Like making a club sandwich there is an order to how these four pillars fit together.

Dharma and Moksha are the bread slices in which the goodies of your sandwich lay. Dharma talks about living in accordance with the principles that uphold life and the world. It ultimately talks about the personal spiritual responsibility and duties we all have to the world we live in. I remember when I lived in the Caribbean I wanted to pick a medicinal herb. As soon as my fingers reached for the herb I was stopped in my tracks. "Did you ask permission from the plant to pick it?" said the voice of the owner looming behind me. "No," I said a little surprised. "Well you have to ask the plants permission to pick its leaves. Oh, and once you done that you must offer a silver coin to the earth to show your gratitude," the owner further informed me.   That was the law of Dharma in practice. Doing the right thing and acting according to universal principles. Today we just take from the Earth without asking her permission for anything, without having gratitude for the things we receive. The result – a consumerist society that has produced a world on "melt down". Through the hard way we are learning that the world and everything in it acts according to fundamental principles which uphold its order.

In the West we love to talk about Freedom. But what is the Freedom that we are talking about? Is it the one that imprisons the soul or liberates it? Moksha is the principle of liberating the soul. It represents the freedom from our negative emotional states and actions. Freedom from these allows us to live a truly happy life. A life free from reactive behavior.

So if Dharma and Moksha are the slices of bread in a beautiful sandwich. Then Artha (being self reliant through earning an income) and Kama (Pleasure of love and human enjoyment) are the scrumptious fillers. The concept of Artha is easy to grasp. For we all love the idea of being self reliant and earning an income to afford us the things we did for our lives. When we cannot look after ourselves in this way we understandably become frustrated, down and depressed. Kama is something we all love. We all love to enjoy ourselves and experience the pleasures of love and life. I remember once reading a Native American book on traditional dances. It was big beautiful and colourful. Besides the

174

stunning pictures there was something that really struck me. It was a Native American quote which pointed out "the person who does not dance in life is a person who is not living. They were also a person who suffers from diseases of the mind, body and spirit."

The slices of bread that hold your scrumptious sandwich together ensure that Artha and Kama do not fall out and mess up of your life. As BKS Iyengar reminded us – Dharma and Moksha are the river banks that stop the waters of pleasure, wealth and all the goodies of life from overflowing and destroying our lives.

Ethics

I remember once picking up the Dalai Lama's book and putting it right back again. Why? Because Ethics has always seemed like such a grandiose word to me. It reminded me of cold wooden corridors and old men with bespectacled faces. Now I understand it is because I misunderstood what Ethics really meant. I knew the word "morality". I was grown up with lots of morals. I come from a culture that uses the word "morals" as opposed to "ethics" a lot. But they really are one of the same. Living in a personal and wider world that engages in ethics is crucial to living in a peaceful world. There really is no other way around it. We cannot grow spiritually without living with a growing sense of Ethics. The Yoga word for Ethics is Yama. The concept of Yama is within all traditional scriptures. So what are the Ethics that we should have in life? Yoga says:

Non-violence

Being violent towards someone is to harm them. This harming can be done in the form of words, deeds, thoughts and actions. In Yoga, violence against someone or something is an offense which goes against the universal principle that there is an underlying unity to all things that exist. It is very much like your hand trying to punch your face. They are all part of the same body so why would the hand even consider hurting the face. It just doesn't make any sense. For it is essentially hurting itself.

Truthfulness

According to the sacred Vedic text of Yoga – nothing that is not founded in truth can bear fruit or bring a good result. Yoga Master Iyengar states, "Truth is the soul communicating with the conscience. If the conscience transmits this to the consciousness and then turns it into action, it is as if our acts become divine, because there is not interruption between the vision of the soul and the execution of its acts."

Non-stealing

Non-stealing talks about not taking what belongs to someone else, this includes property, character and their sense of self esteem.

Celibacy

Celibacy can mean the absence of sex, but in a more subtle sense celibacy talks about a sense of faithfulness. If you are with your partner. Celibacy talks about being faithful to him/her. Think about it. Don't extra marital affairs cause endless strife in life, deep human suffering and misery?

Non-covetousness/modesty of lifestyles

Non-covetousness/modesty of lifestyle means to live without excess. According to the ancient sages – living in excess leads to the bondage of the soul to the world of sensuality and possessions. Which goes against the principle of living immensely and powerfully. Also, covetousness damages Mother Earth and all her living beings.

Journey Pages

I know in my case a trip has really been successful, if I come back sounding strange even to myself.
Pico Iyer

Finally

It is my prayer that you have found this journey beneficial to your mind, body and spirit. I pray for this information to continue to be of benefit to all sentient beings and to end the suffering in the world.

In the spirit of one love, I would like to humbly offer these power words which originate from Africa to Asia, Americas and Europe,

Ashe, Aho, Namaste, Amen and Om Mani Padme Hum.

And may it be so.

You may discover more about me and my work on www.yeyeosuncom

Achikeobi-Lewis, Ezolaagbo. Dreamtime Awakening. Naked Truth Press, 2009.

Achikeobi, Ezolaagbo. A Journey Through Breath. X Press, 1996/

Achikeobi, Ezolaagbo. I Pray for Healing. Naked Truth, 2009.

Aiken, Bill. Seven Sacred Rivers. Penguin Books, 1992.

Barocovcin, Helen. The Way of a Pilgrim. Doubleday, 1997.

Barton, Robert. The Oceans. London. Aldus Books, 1980.

Batchelor, Stephen. The Tibet Guide. Wisdom Publishers, 1987.

Beal, Merrill. Chief Joseph and the Nez Perce War. University of Washington Press, 1996.

Bennett, Hal and Mike, Samuels. The Well Body Book. Random House, 1973.

Bennett, Zina and Sparrow Susans. Follow Your Bliss. Avon Books, 1990.

Bly, Robert. A Little Book on the Human Shadow. Harper San Francisco, 1988.

Bohm, David. 1957. Causality and Chance in Modern Physics, 1961 Harper edition reprinted in 1980 by Philadelphia: U of Pennsylvania Press

Bohm, David. Causality and Chance in Modern Physics. University of Pennsylvania Press, 1980

Bohm, David. The Special Theory of Relativity. W.A. Benjamin, 1965.

Bohm, David. Wholeness and Implicate Order. Ark paperback Routledge, 1980.

Bolen, Shinoda. The Tao of Psychology. Harper and Row, 1979.

Branden, Nathaniel. How to Raise Your Self-Esteem. Bantam Books, 1987.

Brown, Barbara. Supermind: The Ultimate Energy. Harper and Row, 1986.

Browne, Sylvia. Exploring The Levels of Creation. Hay House, 2006.

Burchac, Joseph. Moons on The Turtle Back: A Native American Year of Moons. Putman and Grossnet Group, 1977.

Burnham, Sophy. A Book of Angels. Ballentine Books, 1991.

Butree, M Julia. The Rhythm of the Redman: In Song, Dance and Decoration. A.S Barnes, 1930.

Cameron, Julia. The Artist Way. G.P. Putmans Sons, 1992.

Carson, Rachel. The Sea Around Us. Oxford University Press, 1961.

Chief Joseph. That All People May Be One People, Send Rain to Wash The Face of The Earth. Mountain Meadow Press, 1995.

Cleary, Thomas and Sartaz, Aziz. Twilight Goddess: Spritual Feminism and Feminine Spirituality. Shambala, 2002.

Coleman, Daniel, Ecological Intelligence. Broadway Books, 2009.

Cousins, Norman. The Healing Heart. Avon. Books, 1984.

Cross, John. Acupuncture and Chakra Energy System. North Atlantic Books, 2008.

Demott, Barbara. Dogon Mask. UMI Research Press, 1971.

Eckart, Edona. Bengal Tiger. Children's Press, 2003.

Eckart, Edona. Bengal Tiger. Children's Press, 2003.

Emoto, Masaru. The True Power of Water. Atria Books, 2003.

Fitzgerald, Michael. Yellowtail, Crow Medicine Man and Sun Dance Chief. University of Olkahoma Press, 1991.

Fitzgerald, Michael. Yellowtail, Crow Medicine Man and Sun Dance Chief. University of Olkahoma Press, 1991.

Frankhauser Jerry. The Power of Affirmations. Coleman Graphics, 1983.

Gandhi, Mahatma. Peace. Blue Mountain Arts. Inc.,2001.

Gennep, Arnold. The Rites of Passage. University of Chicago Press, 1960.

Ghanaian Festivals:www.gsu.edu/afinijws/emmal/html

Gibbons, Boyd. "Do We Treat Our Soil Like Dirt?". National Geographic, 1984, pp 350-390.

Gore, Al. Earth in Balance: Ecology & The Human Spirit. Houghton Mifflin, 1992

Gray, Martin. Sacred Earth. Sterling Publishing, 2007.

Gribbin John. Our Changing Planet.Thomas Y. Crowell Co., 1977.

H. Ronald, Bailey. Gacier. Time-Life Books, 1982.

Hall, Judy. The Encyclopedia of Crystals. Octopus Publishing, 2006.

Hawkins, Stephen. The Universe In a NutShell. Bantam Books, Nov 2001.

Holika: www.indiaexpress.com/rangolia/holi/html

Huxley, A. The Doors of Perception. Harper & Row, 1970.

Janganatha, panditraja. The Flow of the Ganges Ganga Lahari. Indica Books, Varanasi, 2007.

Jansem, Eva. The Book of Hindu Imagery. Weisner Books, 1993.

Jansem, Eva. The Book of Hindu Imagery. Weisner Books, 1993.

Jones, Christopher. Big Ice. Publish America, 2003.

Jung, Carl. Man and His Symbols. Dells, 1968.

Jung, CJ. The Structure and Dynamics of the Psyche. RFC. Hull, Vol 8 by Collected Works. Princeton University Press, 1960.

Komfield, Jack. The Path with Heart. Bantam, 1993.

Lama, Dalai Lama. The Dalai Lama's Book of Love and Compassion. Thorsons, 2002.

Leshan, Lawrence. How to Meditate. Boston: Little Brown, 1974.

Lewis and Jordon. Creek Indian Medicine Ways. University of New Mexico. Albuquerque, 2002.

Lewis, C.S. Miracles. Macmillian, 1947.

Lewis, Ray. Choosing Your Career, Finding Your Vocation. Paulist Press. 1989.

Lidell, Lucy. The Sivananda Companion to Yoga. Fireside Book, Simon & Schuster, inc., 1983.

Lilly, Sue and Lilly Simon. Healing with Crystals & Chakra Energies. Annes Publishing Ltd, 2003.

Locke, Steven and Douglas, Collison. The Healer Within. Dutton, 1986.

LockHart, R.A. "Cancer in Myth and Dream". An Annual of Archetypal Psychology and Jungian Thought, 1977: 1-26.

Loy Krathong Festival: www.geocites.com/siamsmile 365/loigratongl/html

Marchant, Kerena, Sloan Frank, Gryspeeroff Rebecca. The Book of Hindu Festivals. Raintree, 2001.

Mckay, Alex. The History of Tibet. Routledge, 2005.

Mindell, A. Working with the Dreaming Body. Routledge & Kegan Paul, 1985.

Monibot, George. Heat,. Allen Lane Penguin Press, 2006.

Moore, Patrick . Travellers in Space and Time. Doubleday and Company, Inc., 1984

Moore, Thomas. Care of the Soul. Haper Perennial, 1992.

Moorey, Teresa. Secrets of Moon Astrology. A Godsfield Book, 2006.

Neihart, G John. Black Elk Speaks. University of Nebraska Press, 1988.

Olson, Carl. The Book of the Goddess Past and Present. Crossroad, 1986.

Oyle, Irving. The Healing Mind. Pocket Books, 1975.

Pais Abraham. "Subtle is the Lord": The Science and Life of Albert Einstein. Oxford University, 1982.

Peck, Scott. The Road Less Traveled. Simon & Schuster, 1978.

Pierre, Mark and Long Soldier, Tilda. Walking in The Sacred Manner. Touchstone, 1995.

Pollard III, John. Self Parenting. Generic Human Studies Publishing, 1987.

Poole, Robert. EarthRise: How man First Saw The Earth. Yale University Press, 2008.

Post, Laurens. The Lost World of The Kalahari. William Morrow, 1958.

Postal, Sandra. Pillars of Sand. WW.Norton Company, 1999.

Ravern, Hazel. Crystal Healing. Raven & Co Publishing, 2000.

Robinson, Jonathan. Shortcuts to Bliss. Conari Press, 1998.

Rocks and Minerals. Parragon, 2008.

Roman, Sanaya and Duane Packer. Creating Money. H.J. Kramer, 1988.

Siegal, Bernies. Peace, Love & Healing. Haper & Row Publishers, 1989.

Simon, Sidney. Setting Unstuck: Breaking Through Barriers of change. Warner Books, 1988.

Some Patrice, Malidoma. Off Water and The Spirit, Penguin. 1995.

Standing Bear, Luther. The Land of the Spotted Eagle. Houghton Mifflin, 1933.

Starhawk. The Spiral Dance. Harper and Rows, 1997.

Stovall, Jim. The Ultimate Shift. River Oak, 2001.

Struthers, Jane. Working with Aura. Godsfield Press, 2006.

Sumiyoshi, S, ed.Nigerian Culture and Customs: A Walk Through Time. Koemar, 1996.

Suzuki, David and MC Connell, Amanda. The Sacred Balance. Greystone Books, 2002.

The Kwatuitl Winter Ceremony: www.geocites.com/wilow1 d/winter.html

Tibetan Festivals: www.accesstibettour.com/tibetan-festivals/html

Tzu, Lao. Tao Te Ching. Penguin, 1963.

Vanbeek, Walte. Dogon: Africa's people of the Cliff. Harry N. Abrams, 2001.

Wade, Davis. Light at The Edge of The World. Vancouver: Douglas & McIntyre, 2002.

Walsh, Roger. The Spirit of Shamanism. J.P Tancher, 1990.

Weiner, Jonathan. Planet Earth. Bantam Books, 1986.

Whitfield Charles. Healing The Inner Child Within. Health Communications, 1987 Iyengar, BKS. B.K.S. Light on Life. Rodale, 2008

www.ingramcontent.com/pod-product-compliance
Lightning Source LLC
LaVergne TN
LVHW061223060426
835509LV00012B/1402

* 9 7 8 0 9 5 4 2 0 6 6 4 2 *